WRITING

W9-BZQ-722

Grade 1

Table of Contents

Writing
Grade 1

Credits:
McGraw-Hill Children's Publishing Editorial/Production Team
Vincent F. Douglas, B.S. and M. Ed.
Tracey E. Dils
Jennifer Blashkiw Pawley
Teresa A. Domnauer
Tanya Dean
Amy Mayr

Big Tuna Trading Company Art/Editorial/Production Team
Mercer Mayer
John R. Sansevere
Erica Farber
Brian MacMullen
Matthew Rossetti
Linda Hayward
Kamoon Song
Soojung Yoo

Mc Graw Hill Children's Publishing

1-57768-851-1

3 4 5 6 7 8 9 10 POH 06 05 04 03

The McGraw-Hill Companies

WELCOME TO CRITTERVILLE!

Spider

Frog

Grasshopper

Mouse

Little Critter

Little Sister

Dad

Kitty

Mom

Blue

Gator

Bat Child

Gabby

Bun Bun

Tiger

Maurice

Molly

Malcolm

Alphabet Review

Trace these capital letters.

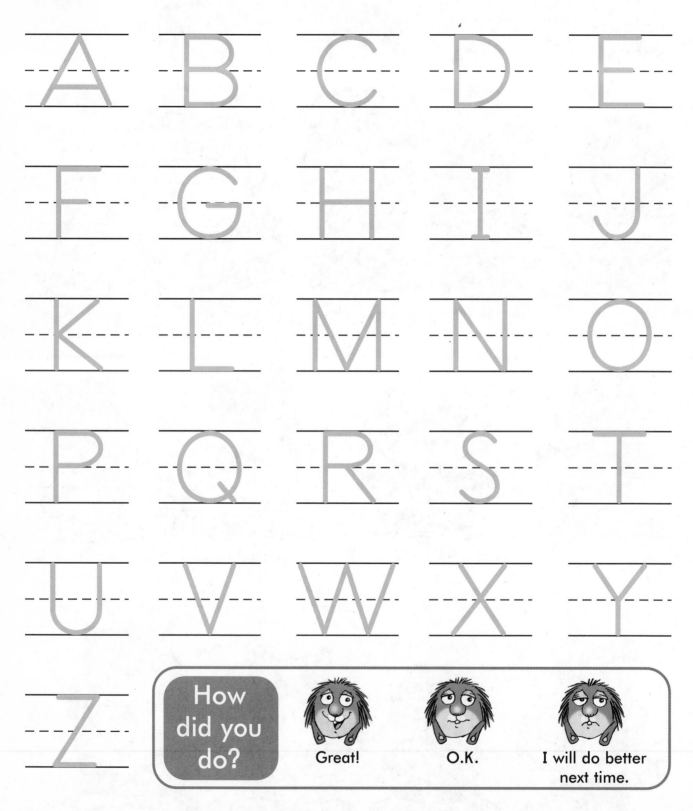

A B C D E

F G H I J

K L M N O

P Q R S T

U V W X Y

Z

How did you do?

Great!   O.K.   I will do better next time.

Trace these lowercase letters.

a b c d e

f g h i j

k l m n o

p q r s t

u v w x y

z

Remember good work habits:
- Find a quiet place to work. No TV.
- It is best to sit at a table.
- Make sure you have good lighting.

Missing Letters

Write the missing lowercase letters. Use your best handwriting.
Use the alphabet below to help you.

a b c

a b

b c

d f

e f

d e

g i

g h

h i

a b c d e f g h i j k l m

Keep going! Write the missing lowercase letters.

j   l   m   n

    k   l   m   o

    j   k   n   o

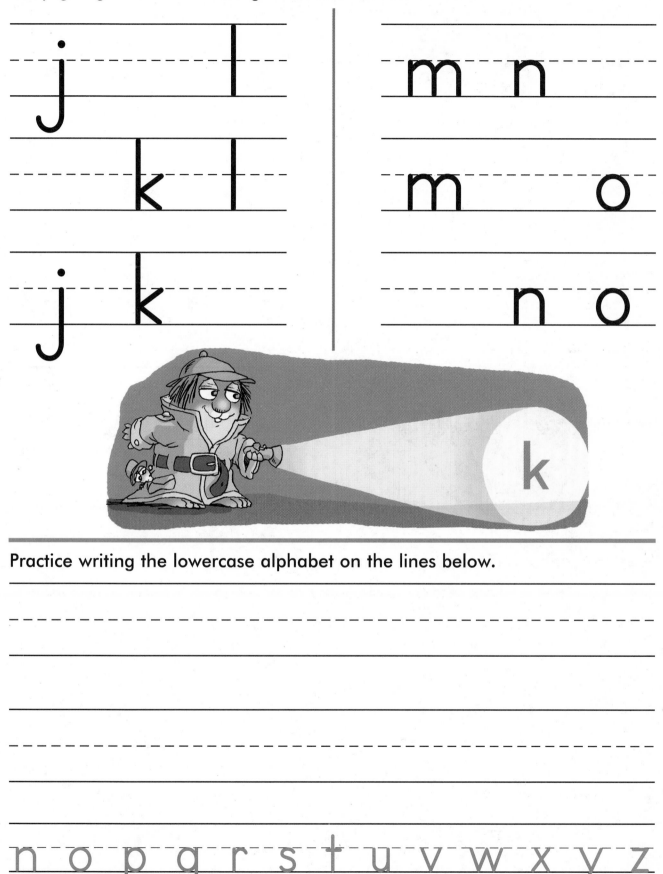

k

Practice writing the lowercase alphabet on the lines below.

n o p q r s t u v w x y z

Keep going! Write the missing lowercase letters.

p   q   s   u   v

     q   r   s   t   u

p   r   s   t   v

                              t   u   v

Practice writing the lowercase alphabet on the lines below.

a b c d e f g h i j k l m

Keep going! Write the missing lowercase letters.

x y z

w x z

w x y

w y z

Handwriting Check

Look at your handwriting on the previous pages.
❑ Did you take your time?

❑ Are the letters sitting on the lines?

❑ Do your tall letters touch the top line?
❑ Do your small letters fit between the dotted line and the lower line?

How did you do? (circle one)

Great!    O.K.

I will do better next time.

n o p q r s t u v w x y z

More Missing Letters

Write the missing capital letters. Use the alphabet below to help you.

A B C

A B

B C

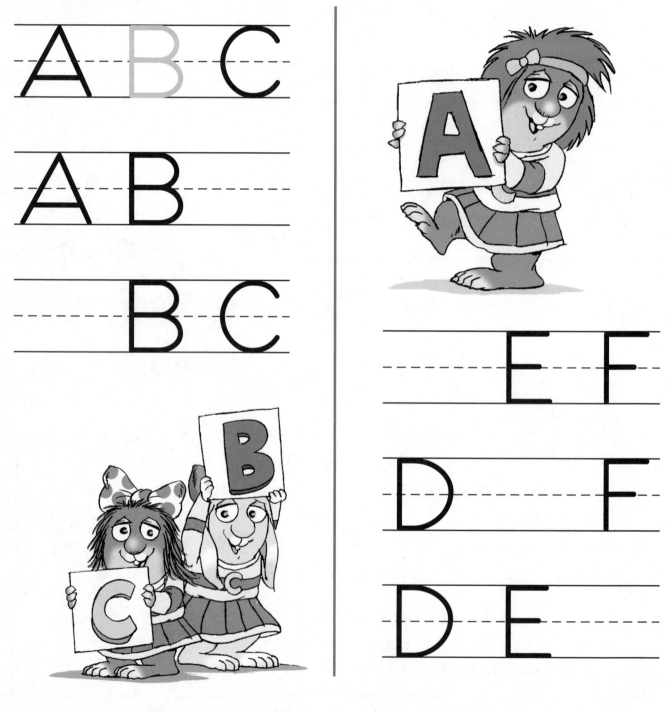

E F

D F

D E

Keep going! Write the missing capital letters.

G H _ _ _

G _ H I

_ G _ H I

_ J _ L

J K L

J _ K _

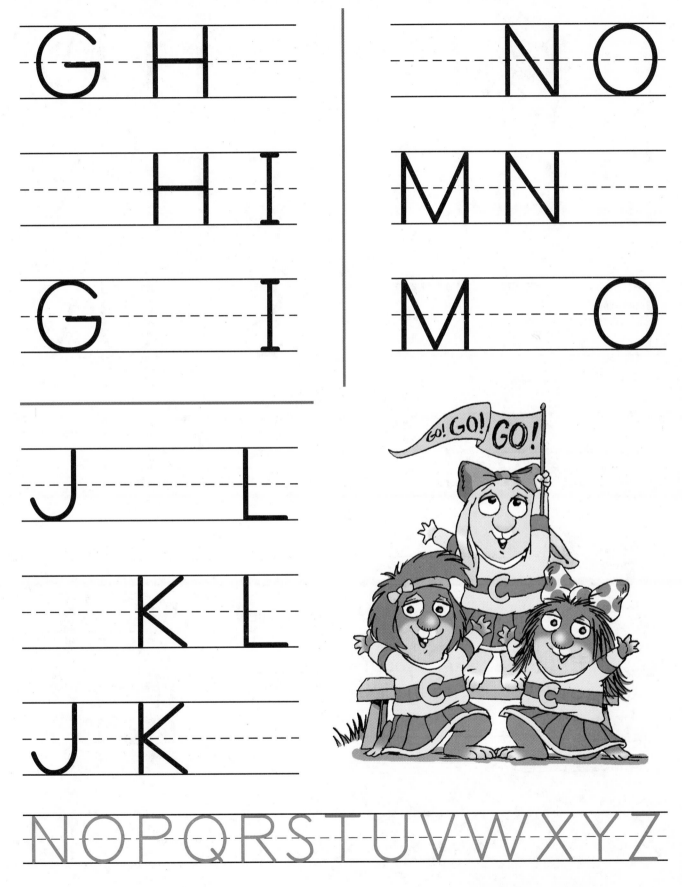

N O

M N _

M _ O

N O P Q R S T U V W X Y Z

Keep going! Write the missing capital letters.

P Q

P R

Q R

T U V

S T V

S U V

S T U

• Did you take your time?

• Are your letters sitting on the line?

A B C D E F G H I J K L M

Keep going! Write the missing capital letters.

W X Y

W ___ Y Z

W X ___ Z

___ X Y Z

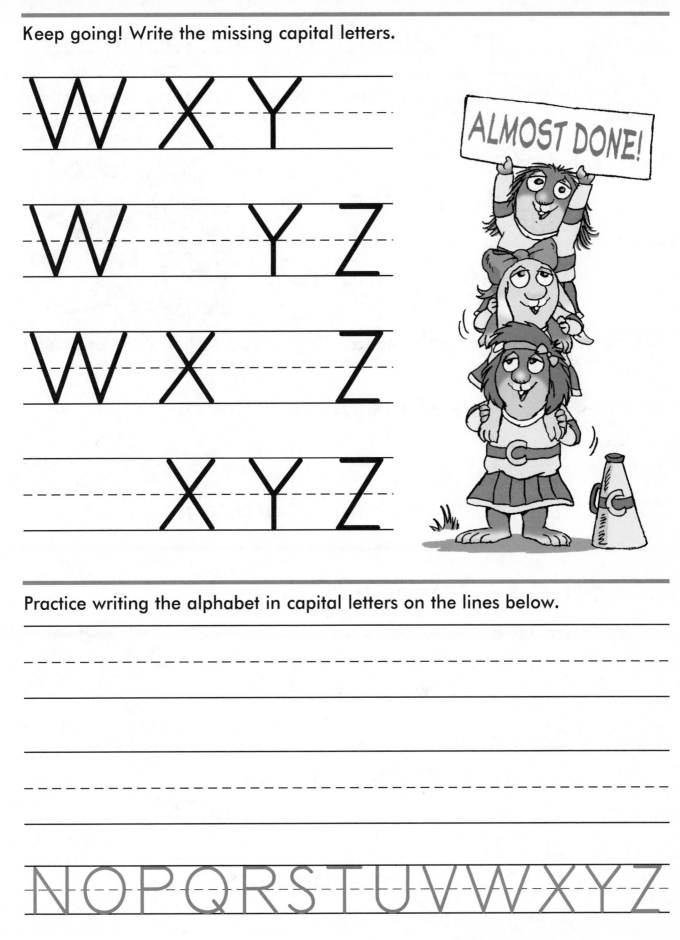

ALMOST DONE!

Practice writing the alphabet in capital letters on the lines below.

N O P Q R S T U V W X Y Z

Capitalization: Sentences

The first word of a sentence always begins with a capital letter.

Incorrect:

the kite is in the tree.

Correct:

The kite is in the tree.

Rewrite the first word of each sentence. Write a capital letter at the beginning of each sentence.

it   is stuck on a branch.

_____

- - - - - - - - - - -

_____ is stuck on a branch.

here   comes a bird.

_____

- - - - - - - - - - -

_____ comes a bird.

the   bird gets the kite.

_____

- - - - - - - - - - -

_____ bird gets the kite.

Proofreader's Toolbox
Use this mark ≡ underneath a letter to show that it needs to be a capital letter.

Make your proofreader's mark ≡ under each letter that should be a capital letter. Write the capital letter above each one.

Example: g̲abby lives near Little Critter.

they go to Critterville Elementary.

they are good friends.

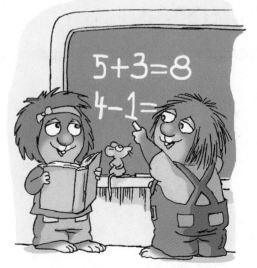

miss Kitty is their teacher.

both of them like math.

Capitalization: People's Names

A person's (or a critter's) name always begins with a capital letter. The other letters in the name are lowercase.

Maurice and Molly are writing their names.
They both remembered to use a capital
letter at the beginning.

Trace the letters in their names.

Maurice   Molly

Now write their names on the lines below.

_____   _____

- - - - - - - - - - - -   - - - - - - - - - - - -

_____   _____

Draw a picture of yourself. Write your name on the line below.
Remember to use a capital letter at the beginning of your name.

_____

- -

_____

Here is Little Critter's list of family names. Trace each name. Then write each name again on the line.

Little Sister

Mom

Dad

Write the names of people in your family. Use a capital letter at the beginning of each name and lowercase letters for the rest of the name.

Parents: If your child needs support, write the family names on the dotted lines and have your child trace your writing. Or, write the names on another piece of paper, and have your child write the names on this page.

Capitalization: Pets' Names

A pet's name always begins with a capital letter.

Little Critter has a dog named Blue.

Trace the letters in Blue's name.

Blue

Write Blue's name on the line below.

Draw a picture of a pet. It can be a real pet or a silly pet you make up. Write your pet's name on the line below. Use a capital letter at the beginning of the pet's name.

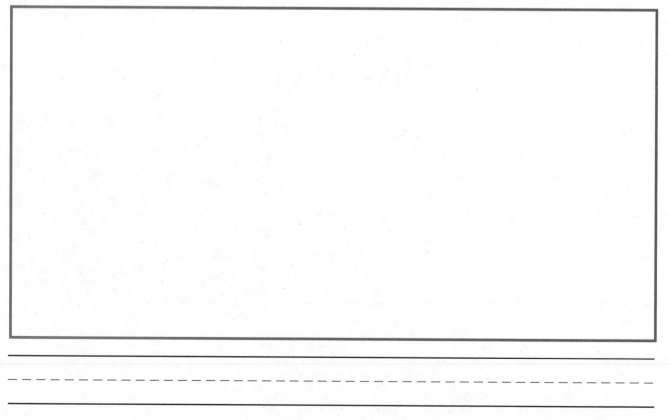

Here are five pet names and five pets. Use your proofreader's mark ≡ to show which letters should be capitalized. Write the capital letter above. Draw a line to match each name to the picture of the animal it belongs to. Hint: The pet names describe the pets.

B
blue
≡

crawly

froggy

kitty

squeaky

hopper

Naming Words — Nouns

A word that names a person, place, or thing is called a **noun.**

person

boy
student
brother

place

Critterville
school
clubhouse

thing

kite
goldfish
sock

Can you name these nouns?

person

_____

_ _ _ _ _ _ _ _ _ _

_____

place

_____

_ _ _ _ _ _ _ _ _ _

_____

thing

_____

_ _ _ _ _ _ _ _ _ _

_____

Here are some nouns. Read the nouns. Then write the name of each thing on your own.

cow

_____
- - - - - - - - - - - - - - - - - - -
_____

web

_____
- - - - - - - - - - - - - - - - - - -
_____

spoon

_____
- - - - - - - - - - - - - - - - - - -
_____

doll

_____
- - - - - - - - - - - - - - - - - - -
_____

truck

_____
- - - - - - - - - - - - - - - - - - -
_____

Naming Words — Nouns

Little Sister wrote some sentences. But she left out the nouns. Can you fill in the blanks using the word list? Write the best noun for each sentence.

I like to go down the _____.

I made my _____.

I looked out the _____.

My _____ keeps me warm.

The _____ makes me laugh.

Word List

coat   bed

clown   slide   window

Action Words — Verbs

A word that tells what is happening in a sentence is called a **verb**. Verbs are **action words**.

It is field day at Critterville School. There is a lot of action on the field.

Look at the pictures below. Read the action word under each picture.

| jump | skip | run | duck | hop |

In the sentences below, circle the action words.

Little Critter (jumps).

Bun Bun skips.

Tiger runs.

Gator ducks.

Maurice and Molly hop.

Action Words—Verbs

Write an action word in each blank. Use the word list to help you.

Word List
shouts
throws
catches
kicks

Miss Kitty _____, "Ready, set, go!"

Gator _____ the baseball.

Bun Bun _____ the ball to Gabby.

Tiger _____ the soccer ball.

Write two sentences telling what Little Critter and his friends are doing on the playground. Use action words.

Example: Tiger climbs the rope.

1. _____

2. _____

Little Critter made a list of some of his favorite action words. Choose three that you like. Write a sentence using each one.

Word List
play
swim
help
sing
make
find

☆ _____

_____

_____

☆ _____

_____

_____

☆ _____

_____

_____

Adjectives

A word that describes a noun is called an **adjective**. Adjectives tell what something looks like.

Which of these two sentences is more interesting?

Little Critter wears a hat.

Little Critter wears an orange hard hat.

Read the story below or have someone read it to you. Circle the adjectives.

Bun Bun likes to paint with bright colors. Her mom's favorite painting is called The Flower Garden. It is a picture of three yellow flowers, two silly green bugs, and one red rubber ball.

Draw the picture described above.

Fill in each blank with the correct adjective. Use the word list to help you.

Word List					
gray	wooden	striped	floppy	furry	yellow

Little Critter wears a __yellow__ shirt.

Gabby holds a _____ cat.

Molly chooses a _____ dress.

Tiger plays with a _____ bat.

Gator pets a _____ kitten.

Blue has _____ ears.

Challenge: Look outside. Use a practice page in the back of this book to make a list of all the words you would use to describe the weather today. Have a friend or family member help you add to the list. Examples: bright, snowy, cold, cloudy

Adjectives That Compare

Adjectives are words that help us describe and compare things. Add **-er** to an adjective when you compare two things. Add **-est** to an adjective when you compare three or more things.

Little Critter is a fast runner.

Gabby is faster than Little Critter.

Tiger is the fastest runner of all three.

This chart is not finished. Fill in the empty boxes with the correct words.

fast	faster	fastest
short	shorter	shortest
close	closer	closest
	taller	
		hardest
deep		deepest

Write the correct word. Choose one of the words underneath each blank.

Tuesday was _____ .
(hot, hotter, hottest)

Thursday was _____ than Tuesday.
(hot, hotter, hottest)

Saturday was the _____ day of the week.
(hot, hotter, hottest)

The sentences below have some mistakes. Draw lines through each incorrect word and write the correct word above it.

Little Sister's towel is small than Bun Bun's towel.

Little Sister has a loudest voice.

Write a sentence using one of the words from the chart on page 28.

_____

- -

_____

Handwriting Check

Look at your handwriting above.

❏ Are your words sitting on the line?
❏ Did you take your time?
❏ Did you put spaces between your
  words?
❏ Do your tall letters touch the top line?
❏ Do your small letters fit between the
  dotted line and the lower line?

How did you do? (circle one)

Great!

O.K.

I will do better next time.

Color Words

Trace the color words.
Match them to the correct picture.

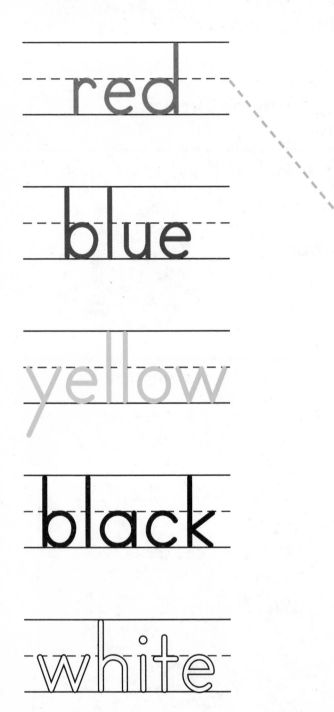

red

blue

yellow

black

white

Color Words

Trace the color words.
Match them to the correct picture.

green

purple

pink

orange

brown

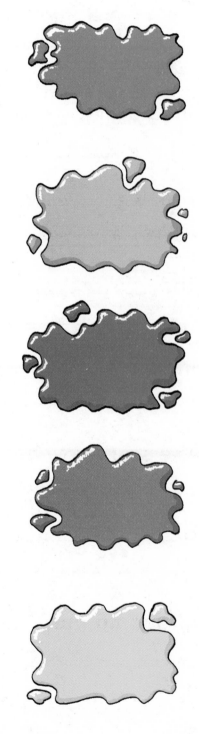

Color words help tell what something looks like.

Which of these two sentences is more interesting?

The pig plays in the mud.

The pink pig plays in the brown mud.

Read all of the sentences first to see how they sound. Then add color words to make the sentences more interesting. Use the color words on pages 30 and 31 to help you fill in the blanks. The first one is done for you.

The ___brown___ cat has a ___green___ ball.

The _____ spider crawled on

the _____ pail.

The scarecrow has an _____ hat and

a _____ shirt.

Grandma put _____ berries in a

_____ bowl.

Number Review

Trace the numbers. Then practice writing the numbers on the lines.

0 1 2 3 4 5 6 7 8 9

0 0

1 1

2 2

3 3

4 4

5 5

6 6

7 7

8 8

9 9

Parent Note: Encourage your child to do this page over several days. Try to do just one line a day.

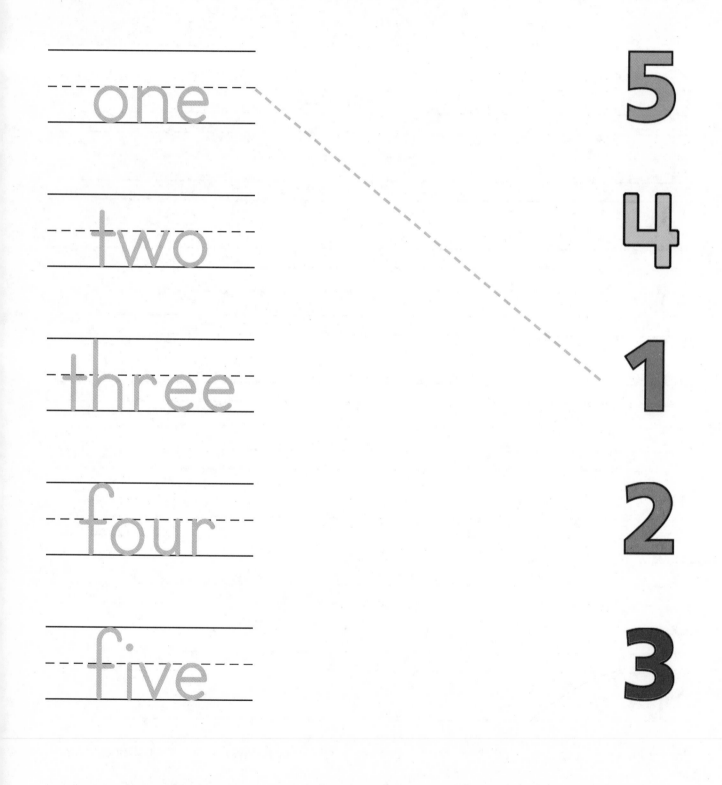

Number Words

Trace the number words.
Match them to the correct numeral.

one

two

three

four

five

5

4

1

2

3

Number Words

Trace the number words.
Match them to the correct numeral.

six

seven

eight

nine

ten

 8

 6

 9

 7

10

Number words help the reader better understand your writing.

Which of these two sentences is clearer?

There were guests at my party.

There were four guests at my party.

Fill in the blanks with the correct number word. Use the number words on pages 34 and 35 to help you. The first one is done for you.

There were _five_ candles on Little Sister's cake.

Little Sister got a shirt with _____

stars on the front.

Gabby gave Little Sister _____ books.

There were _____ balloons in the air.

Everyone got _____ scoops of ice cream.

Ordinal Numbers

Telling the order of people or events will help make your writing clearer.

Little Critter is the first in line.

first	second	third	fourth	fifth
Little Critter	Little Sister	Bun Bun	Gator	Rocky

Use the picture above to fill in the blanks with words from the word list.

Word List				
first	second	third	fourth	fifth

Little Critter is the ___first___ in line.

Bun Bun is the _____ in line.

Little Sister is the _____ in line.

Rocky is the _____ in line.

Gator is the _____ in line.

Antonyms/Opposites

Some words have opposite meanings—these words are called **antonyms**.

Up and down are **antonyms**. They mean the **opposite** of each other.

Little Sister is up **in the air.**
Little Critter is down **on the ground.**

Read the words. Match a word in the left column with its opposite in the right column.

big	dry
best	night
open	worst
day	closed
wet	little
stop	slow
left	go
yes	new
fast	right
old	no

A circus came to Critterville. Little Critter and his friends went to the circus. Circle the **antonyms** in each pair of sentences.

The lions were (inside) a cage.

Little Critter was (outside) the cage.

The large weight lifter lifted 50 pounds.

The small weight lifter lifted 500 pounds.

One trapeze artist soared up.

The other trapeze artist swooped down.

A tall clown walked on stilts.

A short clown got out of a mini car.

Fill in each blank with the proper antonym. Use the word list to help you.

Gabby saw a _____sad_____ clown sitting beside

a _____ clown. Tiger watched the animal

parade. The horses were _____ and the elephants

were _____ . An acrobat flipped _____ and

_____ around the big top.

Word List
sad
forward
slow
happy
fast
backward

Synonyms

Words that have almost the same meaning are called **synonyms**.

Happy and glad are synonyms.

Little Critter is happy to get a new robot.

Little Critter is glad to get a new robot.

One word in the sentence above changed, but the meaning stays the same.

Read the words in the first column below. Circle the word that means almost the same thing as the first word.

gift		present	sock	kite
friend		farmer	pal	author
little		big	happy	small
shy		bashful	mean	tired
smile		run	shake	grin
laugh		hope	giggle	sniff

Match the words that mean almost the same thing.

end	mother
funny	loud
father	unhappy
mom	silly
noisy	dad
sad	begin
start	stop

Read the sentence that Little Critter wrote. On the line below rewrite the sentence using another word for **rest**.

I need to take a rest.

_____

_____

Sound Words

Shhhhh! Can you hear the sound words? Write the sound word next to the picture it goes with. Use the word list below.

Word List
whoosh   moo   pop   honk   roar   woof

woof

_____

_____

_____

_____

_____

Using words that sound like what they mean is called onomatapoeia. Isn't that a fun word to say? [on-o-mah-tah-pea-ah]

Write the sound word next to the picture it goes with. Use the word list below.

Word List

| buzz | tick-tock | bang |
| chirp | quack | croak |

quack

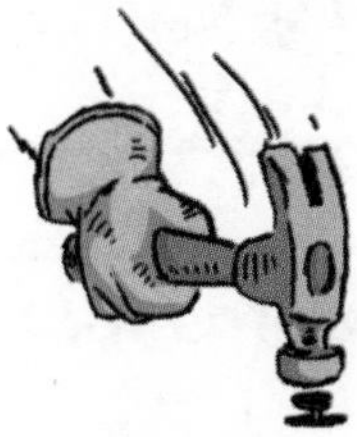

_____

_____

_____

_____

_____

Describing Critters

Little Critter made a list of describing words. These words tell about how he looks and how he feels.

furry	friendly
happy	blue overalls
young	yellow buttons
smart	big eyes

Here are some more describing words. Circle the words that best describe Little Sister.

(girl)	furry
boy	big bow
red overalls	old
happy	grumpy
long hair	two pink hearts

Here are some more describing words. Circle the words that best describe Tiger.

long tail	weak
grumpy	purple pants
round face	orange shirt
black stripes	strong

Can you make a list to describe the critters below? Think of things like size, shape, hair and eye color, and clothing. You can choose words from the word list or try to think of some on your own.

Word List			
spotted	big	long nose	blue bow
green	small	droopy ears	pointy ears
gray	wings	fluffy tail	long tail

Just Me!

Look in a mirror. What do you see? Draw a picture of yourself. Then make a list like Little Critter did at the top of page 44. Write words that tell about how you look, how you dress, and how you feel.

Describing Words

Review: Describing Words

The boy with the cap ran.

The little boy with the blue cap ran fast.

Describing words make your writing more interesting. Describing words tell things like:

what kind?	how many?	which one?
when?	where?	how?

Look at the pictures below. Write two describing words for each picture. Use the word list below.

Word List
muddy   cold   spotted   old   red   two

red

Complete Thoughts

A **sentence** tells a whole idea.

When you write a sentence, make sure it is all there. It will have a beginning and an end. Just a beginning or just an end is not a complete sentence.

Draw a line from each sentence's beginning to its correct ending.

Gabby wanted   taking a nap.

The cookies are   find his bone.

Today the bus   to read.

Blue couldn't   over the fence.

Little Sister is   in the oven.

Tiger jumped   was late.

Punctuation: Periods

Use a **period** to end a complete sentence. A period is like a stop sign.

Little Critter is going hiking with his family.

They are hiking in the woods.

On their hike, Little Critter had a great time. When he got home, he wrote about the hike. Add periods at the end of each sentence.

We saw a deer.

Little Sister counted three squirrels

There was a huge oak tree in the middle of the woods

An acorn dropped on my head

Dad found a bird nest

Mom showed me a caterpillar

Sentence Practice

Little Critter drew some pictures. He wrote a sentence about the first one. Write a sentence about the second picture on your own. Be sure to use some describing words to make your sentence more interesting.

The purple caterpillar crawls along slowly.

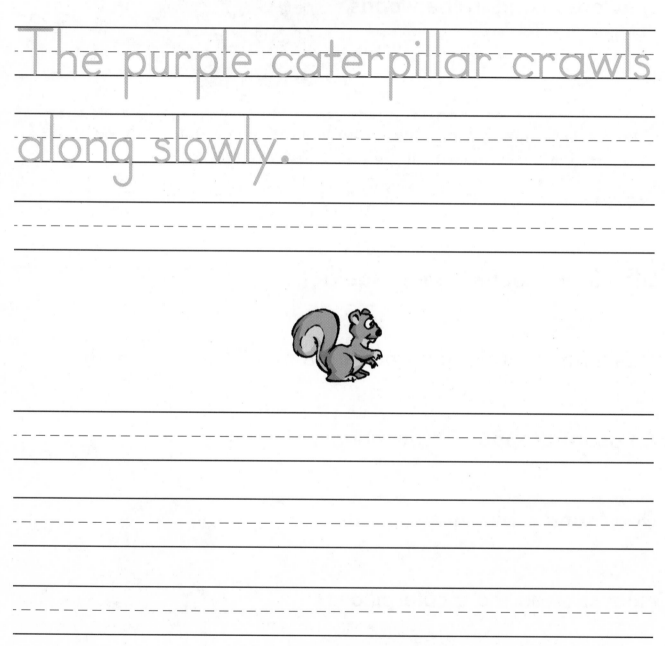

Punctuation: Question Marks

A **question** is a sentence that asks something. Its first word begins with a capital letter. A question ends with a **question mark** (?).

What is worse than finding a worm in your apple?

Finding half a worm.

Trace these question marks. Then write some of your own. Circle your two best question marks.

? ? ? ? ? ? ? ? ?

Bat Child has some more riddles. Add a question mark at the end of each sentence that asks something.

What has a head and a tail and no body

What has hands, but no feet

What has legs, but cannot walk

What runs, but never walks

Punctuation Practice

Write a sentence about this picture.

_____

- -

_____

Write a question about this picture.

_____

- -

_____

Challenge: Write a list of questions that will help you to find out more about someone you already know. Examples: How old are you? What is your favorite food?

Punctuation: Exclamation Points

Sentences that show surprise or excitement end with an **exclamation point** (!). When you read an **exclamation**, your voice should show excitement.

Wow! My tooth came out!

Trace these exclamation points. Then write some of your own. Circle your two best exclamation points.

Little Critter wrote some sentences. Read the sentences or have someone read them to you. Circle the sentences that show excitement. They should end with an exclamation point.

I got a dog for my birthday!

Tomorrow is Monday.

I had a banana for breakfast.

That gorilla ate my banana!

Practice reading each exclamatory sentence with excitement in your voice.

Punctuation Practice

Read Little Critter's story or have someone read it to you. Put three more exclamation points (!) where they belong.

My Lucky Day

One day I was on my way home from school. I was trying to whistle. I had been practicing for a long time, but I could never make a noise. All of a sudden, I could do it! I whistled all the way home.

I played basketball that same day. Our team was tied with the other team. I got the ball and passed it to Gator. He jumped up. Then he dunked the ball through the hoop. We scored the winning basket

I was walking home from the game and I looked down. I found a shiny, new quarter on the ground. Wow It was my lucky day

Punctuation Review

A sentence always begins with a capital letter. It ends with a period (.) or a question mark (?) or an exclamation point (!).

A mouse ran under the table.
Did a mouse run under the table?
Eek! A mouse ran under the table!

Write each sentence. Be sure to use a capital letter at the beginning and a period at the end.

★ i took a red balloon

_____

★ we went to school

_____

★ he played soccer

_____

★ mom found my glove

_____

★ tomorrow is my birthday

_____

★ she rode her bike

_____

Punctuation Review

Remember to use a question mark (?) when your sentence asks something.

Who jumped over the rock?

Write each sentence. Be sure to use a capital letter at the beginning and a question mark at the end.

★ when are we going home

★ are you getting cold

★ how did you learn to whistle

★ will you get my coat

★ can the dog roll over

★ where are my shoes

Punctuation Review

Use an exclamation point (!) when you write a sentence that shows surprise or excitement.

Wait for me!

Write each sentence correctly. Be sure to use a capital letter at the beginning and an exclamation point at the end.

★ watch out

_____

- -

_____

★ don't touch that

_____

- -

_____

★ look at me go

_____

- -

_____

★ give me that right now

_____

- -

_____

★ he won the race

_____

- -

_____

★ you did a great job

_____

- -

_____

Sentence Starters

Write an ending for each of these sentences.

The turtle walked to the

pond.

I sprayed

My book

Riding my

The present

Sentence Starters

Write an ending for each of these sentences.

A big bus took the whole

class to the zoo.

The swing _____

_____

_____

Dad found _____

_____

_____

The truck _____

_____

_____

A bad storm _____

_____

_____

Sentence Endings

Write a beginning for each of these sentences.

The cow lived

_____

_____ in the barn.

_____

_____ as a kitten.

_____

_____ football game.

_____

_____ during class.

_____

_____ in the pool.

Sentence Endings

Write a beginning for each of these sentences.

_____
- -
_____
_____

_____ in the ocean.

_____
- -
_____
- -

_____ secret treasure.

_____
- -
_____
- -

_____ smelled bad.

_____
- -
_____

_____ like a bunny.

_____
- -
_____

_____ in the sky.

Sentence Practice

First, look at each picture. Then write a sentence about each one. Make sure you start with a capital letter and end with a period.

Question and Exclamation Practice

First, look at the pictures. Write two sentences that are questions and two sentences that are exclamations.

Where is Dad going?

Sequencing

Carefully tear out page 65. Cut out the pictures. Match the pictures with the correct sentences. Then glue the pictures to this page.

First, Mom mixed the dough.

Next, Mom cut out the cookies.

Last, she put them in the oven.

Sequencing

Tear out this page. Cut the pictures apart. Put them in order and then glue them onto page 64.

This page is blank for the cutting
activity on the other side.

Sequencing

Tear out this page. Cut the pictures apart. Put them in order and then glue them onto page 69.

This page is blank for the cutting
activity on the other side.

Sequencing

Carefully tear out page 67. Cut out the pictures. Match the pictures with the correct sentences. Then glue the pictures to this page.

Order Words

Order words tell us what came first, next, and last.

First, Mom mixed the dough.

Next, Mom cut out the cookies.

Last, she put them in the oven.

Label the pictures below **first**, **next**, and **last**.

first

-----------   -----------   -----------

-----------   -----------   -----------

Beginning, Middle, and End

All stories have three parts:

| **beginning** | **middle** | **end** |

Little Sister got
out of bed.

She got ready
for school.

The school bus
took her to school.

Here are three sentences that are not in the right order. Write the sentences in order (beginning, middle, and end) to make a story.

Everyone clapped.

Bat Child did a magic trick.

He made a bunny appear.

_____

- -

_____

- -

_____

- -

_____

Using Order Words

Saturday is Little Sister's favorite day of the week. Read her story below and circle the order words you learned on page 70.

First, I help make pancakes. Next, I play all day. Last, I get to stay up until my brother goes to bed.

Using Order Words

Draw a picture about your favorite day of the week. Then write about what you do that day. Be sure to use the order words first, next, and last.

Beginning, Middle, and End

All stories have a beginning, middle, and end. Here are three sentences. They are not in the right order. Write them in order on the lines below to make a story. Then draw a picture of the story.

All of her friends came to the party.

Bun Bun's birthday was Saturday.

They ate cake and played games.

The End

Finish this story.

Little Critter and Dad went fishing. They sat in a boat. They waited and waited. No fish were biting. Then, all of a sudden, Dad felt something pull on his line. It was a huge

_____

- -

_____

- -

_____

- -

_____

- -

_____

- -

_____

The Beginning and Middle

This story has an ending, but it doesn't have a beginning or a middle. Can you write those parts? Look at the picture and word list for ideas.

<table>
<tr><td>Word List</td></tr>
<tr><td>bakery</td></tr>
<tr><td>cookies</td></tr>
<tr><td>delicious</td></tr>
<tr><td>cupcakes</td></tr>
</table>

I Was So Hungry

_____

_____

_____

_____

_____

_____

_____

_____

_____

Last, I went in and bought one to eat on my way home.

The Beginning and Middle

This story has an ending, but it doesn't have a beginning or a middle. Can you write those parts? Look at the picture and word list for ideas.

<table>
<tr><td>Word List</td></tr>
<tr><td>breakfast</td></tr>
<tr><td>cereal</td></tr>
<tr><td>poured</td></tr>
<tr><td>floor</td></tr>
</table>

A Big Mess

_____

- -

_____

- -

_____

- -

_____

- -

_____

- -

Last, Little Critter had to clean up his mess.

Brainstorming

Circle one of the ideas below. Then write down words about that idea.

Idea List

Sports
TV shows
The circus

Animals
Food
Toys

Brainstorming

Circle one of the ideas below. Then write down words about that idea.

Idea List

My Mom   Games
The Park   Soccer
My Neighborhood   Music

Change the Story

Sometimes it is fun to change a story, especially a story everybody knows. Read the story below.

Once upon a time there were three pigs. Each one made his own house. The first pig made his house of straw. The second pig made his house of sticks. The third pig made his house of bricks.

Now write the story again, changing the words in red. Use your imagination. Then read your story aloud to hear the new middle and end you wrote.

_____

- -

_____

- -

_____

- -

_____

_____

- -

_____

_____

Follow the Pictures

Here is a story told only in pictures. Can you follow the pictures and write the story below?

_____

- -

_____

_____

- -

_____

_____

_____

_____

- -

_____

_____

_____

_____

_____

- -

_____

_____

_____

_____

- -

_____

_____

Follow the Pictures

Here is a story told only in pictures. Can you follow the pictures and write the story below?

_____

- -

_____

- -

_____

- -

_____

- -

_____

- -

_____

- -

_____

- -

_____

- -

_____

- -

_____

- -

_____

- -

_____

Just for Fun: Draw and Write

Write a story using one of the ideas below. Then draw a picture to go with your story.

Idea List

The Day I Learned to Fly   When I Grow Up
I Was So Happy   My Biggest Secret

Just for Fun: Draw and Write

Write a story using one of the ideas below. Then draw a picture to go with your story.

Idea List

One Rainy Day   Going to Outer Space
I Was So Scared   If I Could Be Anybody

Just for Fun: Draw and Write

Write a story using one of the ideas below. Then draw a picture to go with your story.

Idea List
If I Had My Own Zoo   My Best Friend
Three Wishes   I Was So Hungry

Writing a Pattern Book

In some cases there is a pattern that the words in a story follow. Only one word changes on each page. Little Critter wrote a pattern book about all the ways he can move. Here are the pages of Little Critter's book.

I can swim.　I can run.

I can roll.　I can slide.

I can jump.　I can climb.

I can walk.　I can skip.

Is this a good title for Little Critter's book?

Things I Can Do

First, write sentences about things you can do. Then read
the directions at the bottom of the page to learn how to
make a book.

_____

I can _____

_____

I can _____

_____

I can _____

_____

I can _____

_____

I can _____

_____

I can _____

Make a Book (Book Activity #1)

1. Take two sheets of blank paper.
2. Fold them in half, so the short sides meet.
3. Have an adult staple the pages together or use
   a sewing machine to stitch up the crease.
4. Write one "I can" sentence on each page.
5. Draw a picture on each page that goes with your
   sentence. Use interesting colors.
6. Write the title on the front cover.
   Now you have a book!

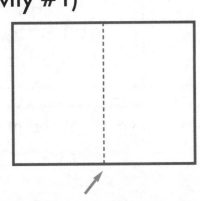

Writing a Pattern Book

In some books there is a pattern that the words follow. Each sentence begins in the same way. Little Critter wrote a pattern book about his birthdays. He used photographs to illustrate the book. Here are some pages from Little Critter's book.

On my first birthday, I had cake all over my face.

On my second, birthday I got a truck.

On my third, birthday I got three balloons.

On my fourth, birthday I had a party.

What do you think the title of Little Critter's book should be?

_____

- -

_____

Writing a Pattern Book

Now it is your turn to write a pattern book. First, think about your own birthday memories. Then, fill in the blanks on page 91. Read the directions below to make your book.

Make a Book (Book Activity #2)

1. Take two sheets of blank paper.
2. Fold them in half, so the short sides meet.
3. Have an adult staple the pages together or use a sewing machine to stitch up the crease.

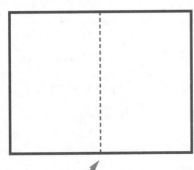

4. Write the title of your book and your name on the front cover.
5. Fill in the sentences on page 91. Then cut out each of the five boxes on page 93.
6. Glue or tape one birthday sentence on each page. You can draw a picture or use photographs to illustrate each page.

Now that you have written a book, you are an author. Read your story to many different people. Then put it in a special place so you can read it again and again.

Start first with your title

My title: _____

Other Ideas for Pattern Books

Write a story about different activities you do on different days of the week.

On Sunday, . . .
On Monday, . . .
On Tuesday, . . .
On Wednesday, . . .
On Thursday, . . .
On Friday, . . .
On Saturday, . . .

On Monday, I go to karate after school.

Write a story about the activities you like to do during the different seasons of the year.

In the spring, . . .

In the summer, . . .

In the fall, . . .

In the winter, . . .

In the fall, I like to jump in the leaves.

Think about what you will be like in the future.

When I am ten years old, . . .

When I am sixteen years old, . . .

When I am twenty years old, . . .

When I am forty years old, . . .

When I am sixty years old, . . .

When I am one hundred years old, . . .

When I am one hundred years old, I will go fishing every day.

Writing a Pattern Book

Make a Book (Book Activity #2)

On my first birthday, _____

_____

_____

On my second birthday, _____

_____

_____

On my third birthday, _____

_____

_____

On my fourth birthday, _____

_____

_____

On my fifth birthday, _____

_____

_____

This page is blank for the cutting
activity on the other side.

Parent Directions for Little Critter Saves the Day

Make a Book (Book Activity #3)

1. Carefully tear out pages 95-98.
2. Fold them in half, so the short sides meet and the picture of Little Critter is on the front cover.
3. You can staple the pages along the folded edge or sew up the crease, using a sewing machine.

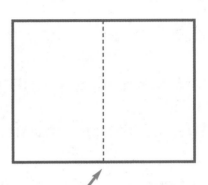

4. Read the sentences to your child. Have your child think of a word to fill in each blank. There is a suggestion for the type of word your child should use underneath each blank.

   For example:

   Little Critter saw ___six___ ___zebras___ at the zoo.
                  (number) (animal)

5. Have your child draw a picture for each page. Encourage your child to use lots of colors and to take time with the illustrations.

Keep the book in a special place. Reread the book often to help your child develop good reading skills.

Story Review

Parent Directions:
Go over this page after you complete the book <u>Little Critter Saves the Day</u>. Read the questions and answers and have your child circle the best answer to each question.

What happens at the beginning of <u>Little Critter Saves the Day</u>?

Little Critter turns into a superhero.

Little Critter is visiting the animals at his grandparents' farm.

Little Critter is dreaming.

What happens in the middle of the story? What is the problem?

Little Critter, the superhero, tries to save Critterville.

Little Critter has a bad dream.

Little Critter notices that one of the animals is missing.

How does the story end? How is the problem solved?

The animal follows Little Critter to its pen.

Little Critter wakes up.

Little Critter saves Critterville and is famous.

94   Creative Writing

Little Critter Saves the Day

by _____

Finally, the _____ came
(missing animal)

walking toward the

_____ . The _____ right
(vegetable)   (animal)

followed Little Critter

back to its pen. Little Critter

helped save the day! Little

Critter and Grandpa

celebrated by having a

_____ .
(sweet treat)

Little Critter went to his grandparents' farm. He saw a

_____ _____ .
(color)   (animal)

Little Critter walked around the field. He yelled, "Here,

_____ !"
(name)

2

7

Grandpa asked Little Critter to help find the missing animal. He gave Little Critter a

_____ (vegetable)

to give to the

_____ (animal).

Next, he went to see the

_____ (animal). Grandma and Grandpa have

_____ (number) of

them!

Then Little Critter had lunch. After lunch, Little Critter went to

Grandma made _____ . see the _____ . But it was
              (food)   (animal)

It was delicious.   gone!

4   5

Write Your Own Story

Answer the questions below. They will help you plan your story.

What can happen at the beginning of your story?
This is a good place to introduce the people in your story and to tell where those people are.

_____

_____

_____

_____

_____

Next, what will happen in the middle of your story? This is a good place to introduce the problem in your story.

_____

_____

_____

_____

_____

How will your story end? How will the problem be solved?

_____

_____

_____

_____

_____

Once you write down your thoughts, you can make a book. Look at page 87 for suggestions on how to make a book. You can even cut your pages into a special shape. For example: If there is a balloon in your story, cut the pages in the shape of a balloon.

Writing Lists

Making a list is one way to report information or record your thoughts. Little Critter's mom made a list for the grocery store. This is what she wrote.

Grocery List
- milk
- cheese
- bread
- juice
- apples
- cookies

Writing a list is a great way to get ideas for a story. Little Sister made a list of things outside her window. Can you help her finish the list? Use the words from the word list to help you. Be careful — some of the words don't make sense!

Things in my backyard
- trees
- clouds
- squirrel

_____

_____

_____

_____

_____

Word List

airplane	birds
spaceship	grass
dinosaur	leaves
flowers	giraffe

Now Make Your Own Lists

Make a list of your favorite foods. Try to think of five things you really like to eat.

_____

_____

_____

_____

_____

_____

_____

_____

Make a list of your favorite toys or games. Try to think of five toys or games you really enjoy.

_____

_____

_____

_____

_____

_____

_____

_____

Challenge: Use the practice pages in the back of this book to make other lists. Some ideas for lists are:
- things that make you happy
- people you know
- your favorite summer activities
- your favorite stories

- things to buy at the store
- all the animals you can think of
- your favorite movies
- new ice cream flavors

Friendly Letters

Read Little Critter's letter to you below. Look at the four different parts that make up a friendly letter.

1) Date:
Begin with a date at the top. Always use a capital letter for the name of the month.

2) Greeting:
Start your greeting with **Dear**. Then write the name of the person you are writing to. Begin each word with a capital letter.

3) Body:
The body of a letter is what you want to say. Use capital letters to begin each sentence.

4) Closing:
You end the letter with a closing and your name. Use a capital letter to begin the closing. Your name should start with a capital letter, too.

September 19, 2001

Dear Reader,

My name is Little Critter. I have a younger sister. Her name is Little Sister. I have a dog named Blue. After school I like to play baseball. What do you like to do after school?

Sincerely,
Little Critter

Parts of a Friendly Letter

Miss Kitty is naming the parts of a friendly letter.

May 2, 2001 ← date

Dear Molly, ← greeting

    I had a good time at your sleep over. Your mom makes the best brownies. The next time, you can come to my house. Thanks again. ← body

        Your friend, ← closing

        Little Sister ← signature

Name the five parts of the letter below:

January 3, 2001 ← date

greeting → Dear Grandpa,

    I had a great time visiting your farm last week. You have a lot more animals than I remembered. I hope I can come for another visit soon. ← body

closing →   Love,

        Little Critter ← signature

Now it is your turn. Write a letter to Little Critter. Tell him at least two things about yourself. Don't forget to use capital letters.

_____
- - - - - - - - - - - - - - -
_____ , _____
(Date)

_____
- -
_____ ,
(Greeting)
_____
- -
_____
_____
_____
_____
- -
_____
(Body)
- -
_____ ,
(Closing)
- -
_____
(Signature — your name)

Checklist:
I used capital letters for the:
- ❏ date
- ❏ greeting
- ❏ beginning of each sentence
- ❏ closing
- ❏ names

Write a friendly letter to your best friend. Tell your friend about your weekend. Be sure to include all the parts of a letter.

_____

- - - - - - - - - - - - - - - - - -

_____ , _____
(Date)

_____

- - - - - - - - - - - - - - - - - -

_____ ,
(Greeting)

_____

- - - - - - - - - - - - - - - - - -

_____

_____

- - - - - - - - - - - - - - - - - -

_____

- - - - - - - - - - - - - - - - - -

(Body)

- ,

_____
(Closing)

- - - - - - - - - - - - - - - - - -

_____
(Signature — your name)

Checklist:
I used capital letters for the:
- ❑ date
- ❑ greeting
- ❑ beginning of each sentence
- ❑ closing
- ❑ names

Thank You Notes

A **thank you note** is really just a short letter. It tells someone thank you for something. It could be for a gift, a favor, or something nice he or she did.

When you write a thank you note, be sure to include:

★ the date you are writing the note
★ the person's name in the greeting
★ what you are thanking the person for
★ your name after the closing

Here is a thank you note to complete. Imagine your grandma sent you $10 for your birthday. Be sure to tell her what you plan to use the $10 for in your note.

<pre>
                                    _____
                                    - - - - - - - - - - - - - - - -
                                    _____,_____
                                              (Date)

         _____
         - - - - - - - - - - - -
Dear _____,_____

         _____
         -
_____
- -
_____
- -
_____

                    Love,

                    _____
                    - - - - - - - - - - - - - - - -
                    _____
</pre>

Thank You Notes

Here is another thank you note to complete. This time imagine your neighbor, Mr. Jones, found your lost dog. Thank him for bringing your pet home safely.

_____
_____ ,
(Date)

Dear _____ ,
_____
_____
_____
_____
_____
_____
_____
_____

Your neighbor,

_____
_____

Invitations

An **invitation** is a letter. It asks someone to come to a party or celebration.

Be sure to write:

- ★ the name of the person you are sending it to
- ★ the kind of party it is
- ★ the day and time of the party
- ★ when the party will be
- ★ your address and phone number

Here is an invitation for you to fill in. It is for a birthday party. It will be on Saturday, June 9, at 2:00 p.m. Use your own address and phone number.

Party Time!

To _____

Please come to my _____ party.

It is on _____ at _____ p.m.

My address is _____

My phone number is _____

Hope you can come!

Invitations

Gator wants to invite Little Critter to his pool party. Fill in the invitation below with this information:

pool party
Friday, July 25
1:00 p.m.
at Gator's house

Join Us!

It's a _____ party.

On _____ at _____ p.m.

Come to _____ .

Bring your swimsuit!

Poetry: Rhyming Words

Words that sound alike are called **rhyming words.** Look at each picture below. Say what the picture is. Then look at the word list to find the word that rhymes with the picture word.

Word List

goat	nose	took	bed	name
ride	phone	sock	pen	stop

stop

_____

_____

_____

_____

_____

_____

_____

_____

_____

Creative Writing

Poetry: Rhyming Words

Write the rhyming word next to the picture. Use the word list.

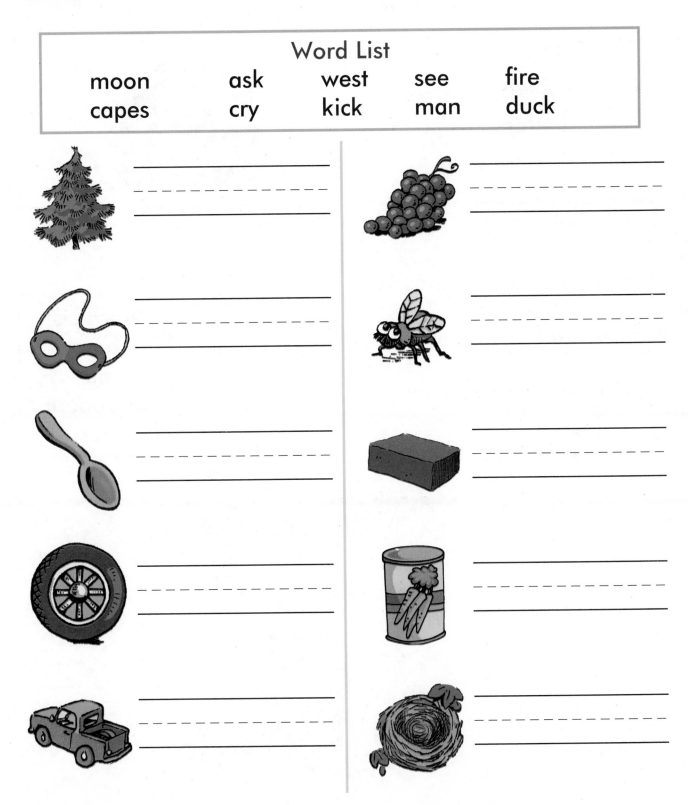

Word List				
moon	ask	west	see	fire
capes	cry	kick	man	duck

Poetry

Poetry is a way to write about something without using a lot of words. Some poems have words that rhyme. Read Little Critter's poem below.

Roses are red,

Violets are blue,

I wrote this poem

Just for you.

Here is another poem. Use the words from the word list to fill in the missing words.

Leaves are falling from the _____.

Leaves are falling down on _____.

I will have to move from _____.

Or I will soon _____.

Word List
here
me
disappear
tree

Here is a rhyming poem about the Critterville kids. Use the word list to help you fill in the missing words.

Little Critter likes to race.

He runs to the starting _____.

Little Sister likes to sing

On her way up in the _____.

Tiger kicks the soccer ball

Hard against the playground _____.

Gabby shouts to all her team,

"Let's go walk across the _____."

Bun Bun likes to jump and land

Safely in a pile of _____.

Gator stops and hears his name.

"Do you want to play a _____?"

Molly likes to take a ride

Down the curvy _____.

Molly's brother slides down last.

Watch out there! Maurice is _____.

Laughing, playing, in the sun—

Recess is the time for _____.

Word List
swing
beam
game
fast
place
wall
sand
slide
fun

Name Poems

Not all poems have to rhyme. Read the poems below. Do you see how Gabby and Tiger used their names to write their poems?

Here is a name poem that Gabby wrote:

Gifted
Adventurous
Bright
Busy
Young girl

Here is a name poem that Tiger wrote:

Terrific
Incredible
Great
Exciting
Runner

Write your name below. Write one letter in each box. Then write a word that begins with each letter—a word that describes you. Write the word on the line beside each box. Use the list on page 115 for ideas.

□ _____

□ _____

□ _____

□ _____

□ _____

□ _____

□ _____

□ _____

Here are some describing words that begin with each letter of the alphabet.

A	amazing	artistic	athletic
B	brave	bubbly	bouncy
C	creative	curious	careful
D	delightful	daring	different
E	energetic	enthusiastic	eager
F	friendly	funny	fair
G	graceful	gentle	glad
H	helpful	honest	happy
I	interesting	inventive	important
J	joking	jolly	joyful
K	kind	kid	keen
L	loud	loving	lucky
M	musical	muscular	mysterious
N	nice	neat	noisy
O	outgoing	original	outstanding
P	patient	peppy	polite
Q	quiet	quick	quite clever
R	responsible	runner	red hair
S	strong	smart	silly
T	talented	trusty	
U	unusual	understanding	
V	vibrant	very sweet	
W	wonderful	weird	
X	expert	excellent	
Y	young	youthful	
Z	zippy	zany	

Writing Shape Poems

Here is a poem Little Critter wrote about stars. He made it more interesting by writing it in the shape of a star.

STARS
Stars are high
In the sky.
When they shine,
They look so fine.
The End.

Stars are high In the sky. When they shine, They look so fine. The end.

Write a poem about clouds. First, make a list of words that you think of when you think of a cloud. Then write them in or around the cloud shape. You can even do this on another piece of paper and glue on cotton balls to make the cloud look fluffy.

Cloud Words

_____
_____
_____
_____
_____
_____
_____

Make a list of words that remind you of a kitten. Use the words to decorate the kitten's face below. You might even try writing the words on the kitten's whiskers.

Kitten Words

_____   _____   _____

_____   _____   _____

_____   _____   _____

Other shapes to try:

Balloon   **Dog**   **Pumpkin**

Writing a Diamond-Shaped Poem

No time to rhyme? Here is a poem for you! Have an adult or a friend work with you.

A **diamante poem** is a poem shaped a little like a diamond. Every line tells more about one topic. The lines do not need to rhyme. Here is one form:

First line: one noun, or word, that names a thing

Second line: two adjectives, or words, that describe that thing

Third line: three verbs with -ing endings

Fourth line: two adjectives

Fifth line: one noun that renames the first noun

Puppy
Little, furry
Wagging, playing, barking
Frisky, friendly
Blue

Tips for Writing Your Own Poem

• Choose an object or creature that really interests you.
• Select adjectives and verbs that tell about your object or creature.
• Read your poem. Are there better words to use?

Write your poem with words that sparkle.

No time to rhyme? Here is a poem for you! Have an adult or a friend work with you.

_____   • one noun, or word, that names a thing

_____, _____   • two adjectives, or words, that describe that thing

_____, _____, _____   • three verbs with -ing endings

_____, _____   • two adjectives

_____   • one noun that renames the first noun

Illustrate your poem here:

Thinking of Things to Write About

Little Critter is making a list of things he can write about. He can use this list when he is searching for an idea for a story.

Things to Write About

★ going to the beach with Grandma

★ spending time at the farm with Grandpa

★ riding the train into the city with Mom

★ going fishing with Dad

★ my pets

★ my favorite teachers

Thinking of Things to Write About

Now it is your turn to start your own list. Remember, you can add to your list whenever you think of something new to write about.

Things to Write About

★

★

★

★

★

★

★

★

★

More Story Ideas

You can also make a list of things you want to write about by drawing a picture to remember. Little Critter drew this picture of a fun, rainy day. Use the space below to draw pictures of things you would like to write about.

More Story Ideas

Use this page to draw or write about more story ideas.

Practice Page

Use this page for extra writing and drawing practice.

Practice Page

Use this page for extra writing and drawing practice.

Practice Page

Use this page for extra writing and drawing practice.

Alphabet Review

Trace these capital letters.

A B C D E
F G H I J
K L M N O
P Q R S T
U V W X Y
Z

How did you do? Great! O.K. I will do better next time.

Trace these lowercase letters.

a b c d e
f g h i j
k l m n o
p q r s t
u v w x y
z

Remember good work habits:
• Find a quiet place to work. No TV.
• It is best to sit at a table.
• Make sure you have good lighting.

Missing Letters

Write the missing lowercase letters. Use your best handwriting. Use the alphabet below to help you.

a b c   d e f
a b c   d e f
a b c   d e f

               g h i
               g h i
               g h i

a b c d e f g h i j k l m

Keep going! Write the missing lowercase letters.

j k l   m n o
j k l   m n o
j k l   m n o

k

Practice writing the lowercase alphabet on the lines below.

a b c d e f g h i j k l m
n o p q r s t u v w x y z
n o p q r s t u v w x y z

Keep going! Write the missing lowercase letters.

p q r   s t u v

p q r   s t u v

p q r   s t u v

          s t u v

Practice writing the lowercase alphabet on the lines below.

a b c d e f g h i j k l m

n o p q r s t u v w x y z

a b c d e f g h i j k l m

Keep going! Write the missing lowercase letters.

w x y z

w x y z

w x y z

w x y z

Handwriting Check

Look at your handwriting on the previous pages.
☐ Did you take your time?

☐ Are the letters sitting on the lines?

☐ Do your tall letters touch the top line?

☐ Do your small letters fit between the dotted line and the lower line?

How did you do? (circle one)

Great!   O.K.

I will do better next time.

n o p q r s t u v w x y z

More Missing Letters

Write the missing capital letters. Use the alphabet below to help you.

A B C   D E F

A B C   D E F

A B C   D E F

A B C D E F G H I J K L M

Keep going! Write the missing capital letters.

G H I   M N O

G H I   M N O

G H I   M N O

J K L

J K L

J K L

N O P Q R S T U V W X Y Z

Keep going! Write the missing capital letters.

S T U V

P Q R   S T U V

P Q R   S T U V

P Q R   S T U V

• Did you take your time?

• Are your letters sitting on the line?

A B C D E F G H I J K L M

Keep going! Write the missing capital letters.

W X Y Z

W X Y Z

W X Y Z

W X Y Z

ALMOST DONE!

Practice writing the alphabet in capital letters on the lines below.

A B C D E F G H I J K L M

N O P Q R S T U V W X Y Z

N O P Q R S T U V W X Y Z

Capitalization: Sentences

The first word of a sentence always begins with a capital letter.

Incorrect:
the kite is in the tree.

Correct:
The kite is in the tree.

Rewrite the first word of each sentence. Write a capital letter at the beginning of each sentence.

it   is stuck on a branch.

It   is stuck on a branch.

here   comes a bird.

Here comes a bird.

the   bird gets the kite.

The bird gets the kite.

Proofreader's Toolbox
Use this mark ≡ underneath a letter to show that it needs to be a capital letter.

Make your proofreader's mark ≡ under each letter that should be a capital letter. Write the capital letter above each one.

Example: G
gabby lives near Little Critter.
≡

T
they go to Critterville Elementary.
≡

T
they are good friends.
≡

M
miss Kitty is their teacher.
≡

B
both of them like math.
≡

5+3=8
4-1=

Capitalization: People's Names

A person's (or a critter's) name always begins with a capital letter. The other letters in the name are lowercase.

Maurice and Molly are writing their names. They both remembered to use a capital letter at the beginning.

Trace the letters in their names.

Maurice   Molly

Now write their names on the lines below.

Maurice   Molly

Draw a picture of yourself. Write your name on the line below. Remember to use a capital letter at the beginning of your name.

Pictures will vary.

Names will vary.

Here is Little Critter's list of family names. Trace each name. Then write each name again on the line.

Little Sister   Little Sister

Mom   Mom

Dad   Dad

Write the names of people in your family. Use a capital letter at the beginning of each name and lowercase letters for the rest of the name.

Names will vary.

Capitalization: Pets' Names

A pet's name always begins with a capital letter.

Little Critter has a dog named Blue.

Trace the letters in Blue's name.

Blue

Write Blue's name on the line below.

Blue

Draw a picture of a pet. It can be a real pet or a silly pet you make up. Write your pet's name on the line below. Use a capital letter at the beginning of the pet's name.

Pictures will vary.

Names will vary.

Here are five pet names and five pets. Use your proofreader's mark ≡ to show which letters should be capitalized. Write the capital letter above. Draw a line to match each name to the picture of the animal it belongs to. Hint: The pet names describe the pets.

B
blue

C
crawly

F
froggy

K
kitty

S
squeaky

H
hopper

Naming Words — Nouns

A word that names a person, place, or thing is called a **noun**.

person — boy
student
brother

place — Critterville
school
clubhouse

thing — kite
goldfish
sock

Can you name these nouns?

person — teacher

place — school

thing — book

Here are some nouns. Read the nouns. Then write the name of each thing on your own.

cow — cow

web — web

spoon — spoon

doll — doll

truck — truck

Naming Words — Nouns

Little Sister wrote some sentences. But she left out the nouns. Can you fill in the blanks using the word list? Write the best noun for each sentence.

I like to go down the __slide__ .

I made my __bed__ .

I looked out the __window__ .

My __coat__ keeps me warm.

The __clown__ makes me laugh.

Word List

coat   bed

clown   slide   window

Action Words — Verbs

A word that tells what is happening in a sentence is called a **verb**. Verbs are **action words**.

It is field day at Critterville School. There is a lot of action on the field.

Look at the pictures below. Read the action word under each picture.

jump   skip   run   duck   hop

In the sentences below, circle the action words.

Little Critter (jumps.)
Bun Bun (skips.)
Tiger (runs.)
Gator (ducks.)
Maurice and Molly (hop.)

Action Words—Verbs

Write an action word in each blank. Use the word list to help you.

Miss Kitty **shouts**, "Ready, set, go!"

Gator **catches** the baseball.

Bun Bun **throws** the ball to Gabby.

Tiger **kicks** the soccer ball.

Word List
shouts
throws
catches
kicks

Write two sentences telling what Little Critter and his friends are doing on the playground. Use action words. Sample answers are given.

Example: Tiger climbs the rope.

1. Gator crawls under a bar.

2. Little Critter hops from tire to tire.

Little Critter made a list of some of his favorite action words. Choose three that you like. Write a sentence using each one.

Sample answers are given.

Word List
play
swim
help
sing
make
find

☆ I can swim across the pool.

☆ Let's sing a song.

☆ I can't find my hat.

Adjectives

A word that describes a noun is called an **adjective**. Adjectives tell what something looks like.

Which of these two sentences is more interesting?

Little Critter wears a hat.

Little Critter wears an orange hard hat.

Read the story below or have someone read it to you. Circle the adjectives.

Bun Bun likes to paint with (bright) colors. Her mom's (favorite) painting is called The Flower Garden. It is a picture of (three) (yellow) flowers, (two) (silly) (green) bugs, and (one) (red) rubber ball.

Draw the picture described above.

Two silly green bugs

Three yellow flowers

One red rubber ball

Fill in each blank with the correct adjective. Use the word list to help you.

Word List
gray   wooden   striped   floppy   furry   yellow

Little Critter wears a **yellow** shirt.

Gabby holds a **gray** cat.

Molly chooses a **striped** dress.

Tiger plays with a **wooden** bat.

Gator pets a **furry** kitten.

Blue has **floppy** ears.

Challenge: Look outside. Use a practice page in the back of this book to make a list of all the words you would use to describe the weather today. Have a friend or family member help you add to the list. Examples: bright, snowy, cold, cloudy

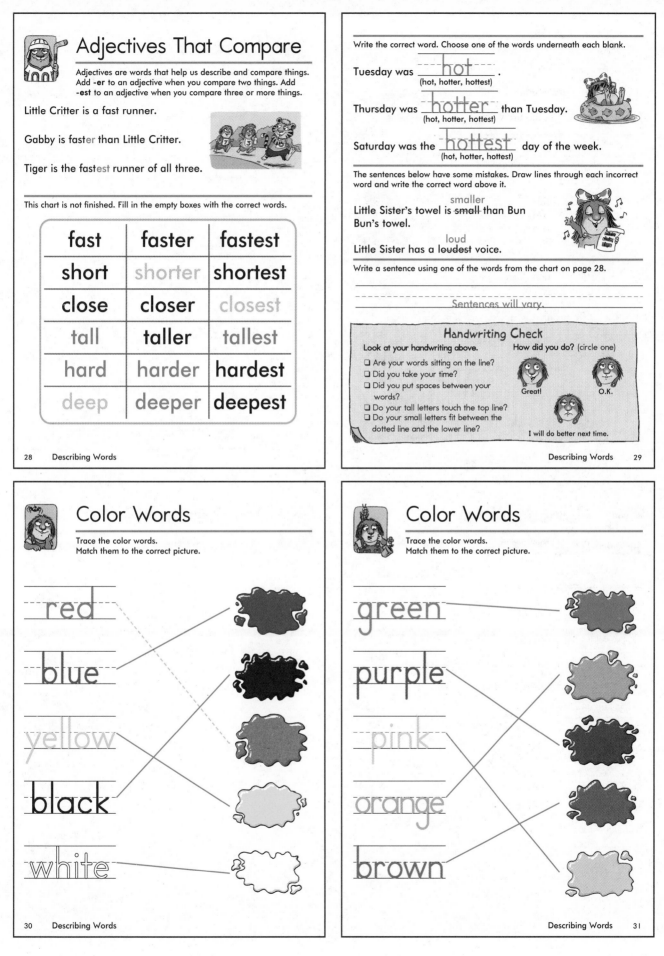

Adjectives That Compare

Adjectives are words that help us describe and compare things. Add **-er** to an adjective when you compare two things. Add **-est** to an adjective when you compare three or more things.

Little Critter is a fast runner.

Gabby is fast**er** than Little Critter.

Tiger is the fast**est** runner of all three.

This chart is not finished. Fill in the empty boxes with the correct words.

fast	faster	fastest
short	shorter	shortest
close	closer	closest
tall	taller	tallest
hard	harder	hardest
deep	deeper	deepest

Write the correct word. Choose one of the words underneath each blank.

Tuesday was ___hot___ .
(hot, hotter, hottest)

Thursday was ___hotter___ than Tuesday.
(hot, hotter, hottest)

Saturday was the ___hottest___ day of the week.
(hot, hotter, hottest)

The sentences below have some mistakes. Draw lines through each incorrect word and write the correct word above it.

smaller
Little Sister's towel is ~~small~~ than Bun
Bun's towel.

loud
Little Sister has a ~~loudest~~ voice.

Write a sentence using one of the words from the chart on page 28.

_____
Sentences will vary.

Handwriting Check

Look at your handwriting above.

☐ Are your words sitting on the line?
☐ Did you take your time?
☐ Did you put spaces between your words?
☐ Do your tall letters touch the top line?
☐ Do your small letters fit between the dotted line and the lower line?

How did you do? (circle one)

Great!   O.K.

I will do better next time.

Color Words

Trace the color words.
Match them to the correct picture.

red

blue

yellow

black

white

Color Words

Trace the color words.
Match them to the correct picture.

green

purple

pink

orange

brown

Color words help tell what something looks like.

Which of these two sentences is more interesting?

The pig plays in the mud.

The pink pig plays in the brown mud.

Read all of the sentences first to see how they sound. Then add color words to make the sentences more interesting. Use the color words on pages 30 and 31 to help you fill in the blanks. The first one is done for you.

The _brown_ cat has a _green_ ball.

The _black_ spider crawled on

the _red_ pail.

The scarecrow has an _orange_ hat and

a _purple_ shirt.

Grandma put _blue_ berries in a

white bowl.

Number Review

Trace the numbers. Then practice writing the numbers on the lines.

0 1 2 3 4 5 6 7 8 9

0 0 0 0 0 0 0 0 0 0

1 | | | | | | | | |

2 2 2 2 2 2 2 2 2 2

3 3 3 3 3 3 3 3 3 3

4 4 4 4 4 4 4 4 4 4

5 5 5 5 5 5 5 5 5 5

6 6 6 6 6 6 6 6 6 6

7 7 7 7 7 7 7 7 7 7

8 8 8 8 8 8 8 8 8 8

9 9 9 9 9 9 9 9 9 9

Parent Note: Encourage your child to do this page over several days. Try to do just one line a day.

Number Words

Trace the number words.
Match them to the correct numeral.

one   5
two   4
three   1
four   2
five   3

Number Words

Trace the number words.
Match them to the correct numeral.

six   8
seven   6
eight   9
nine   7
ten   10

Number words help the reader better understand your writing.

Which of these two sentences is clearer?

There were guests at my party.

There were four guests at my party.

Fill in the blanks with the correct number word. Use the number words on pages 34 and 35 to help you. The first one is done for you.

There were _five_ candles on Little Sister's cake.

Little Sister got a shirt with _four_ stars on the front.

Gabby gave Little Sister _two_ books.

There were _six_ balloons in the air.

Everyone got _three_ scoops of ice cream.

Ordinal Numbers

Telling the order of people or events will help make your writing clearer.

Little Critter is the first in line.

first   second   third   fourth   fifth

Little Critter   Little Sister   Bun Bun   Gator   Rocky

Use the picture above to fill in the blanks with words from the word list.

Word List
first   second   third   fourth   fifth

Little Critter is the _first_ in line.

Bun Bun is the _third_ in line.

Little Sister is the _second_ in line.

Rocky is the _fifth_ in line.

Gator is the _fourth_ in line.

Antonyms/Opposites

Some words have opposite meanings—these words are called **antonyms**.

Up and down are **antonyms**. They mean the **opposite** of each other.

Little Sister is up in the air.
Little Critter is down on the ground.

Read the words. Match a word in the left column with its opposite in the right column.

big   dry
best   night
open   worst
day   closed
wet   little
stop   slow
left   go
yes   new
fast   right
old   no

A circus came to Critterville. Little Critter and his friends went to the circus. Circle the **antonyms** in each pair of sentences.

The lions were (inside) a cage.
Little Critter was (outside) the cage.

The (large) weight lifter lifted 50 pounds.
The (small) weight lifter lifted 500 pounds.

One trapeze artist soared (up.)
The other trapeze artist swooped (down.)

A (tall) clown walked on stilts.
A (short) clown got out of a mini car.

Fill in each blank with the proper antonym. Use the word list to help you.

Gabby saw a _sad_ clown sitting beside

a _happy_ clown. Tiger watched the animal

parade. The horses were _fast_ and the elephants

were _slow_. An acrobat flipped _backward or forward_ and

backward or forward around the big top.

Word List
sad
forward
slow
happy
fast
backward

Synonyms

Words that have almost the same meaning are called **synonyms**.

Happy and glad are synonyms.

Little Critter is happy to get a new robot.

Little Critter is glad to get a new robot.

One word in the sentence above changed, but the meaning stays the same.

Read the words in the first column below. Circle the word that means almost the same thing as the first word.

gift		(present)	sock	kite
friend		farmer	(pal)	author
little		big	happy	(small)
shy		(bashful)	mean	tired
smile		run	shake	(grin)
laugh		hope	(giggle)	sniff

40   Describing Words

Match the words that mean almost the same thing.

end   mother

funny   loud

father   unhappy

mom   silly

noisy   dad

sad   begin

start   stop

Read the sentence that Little Critter wrote. On the line below rewrite the sentence using another word for **rest**.

I need to take a rest.

Sample answer is given

I need to take a nap.

Describing Words   41

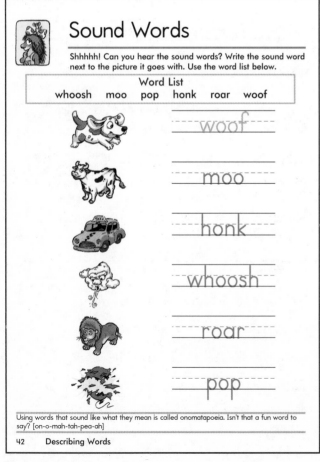

Sound Words

Shhhhh! Can you hear the sound words? Write the sound word next to the picture it goes with. Use the word list below.

Word List
whoosh   moo   pop   honk   roar   woof

woof

moo

honk

whoosh

roar

pop

Using words that sound like what they mean is called onomatopoeia. Isn't that a fun word to say? [on-o-mah-tah-pea-ah]

42   Describing Words

Write the sound word next to the picture it goes with. Use the word list below.

Word List
buzz   tick-tock   bang
chirp   quack   croak

quack

bang

buzz

croak

tick-tock

chirp

Describing Words   43

136

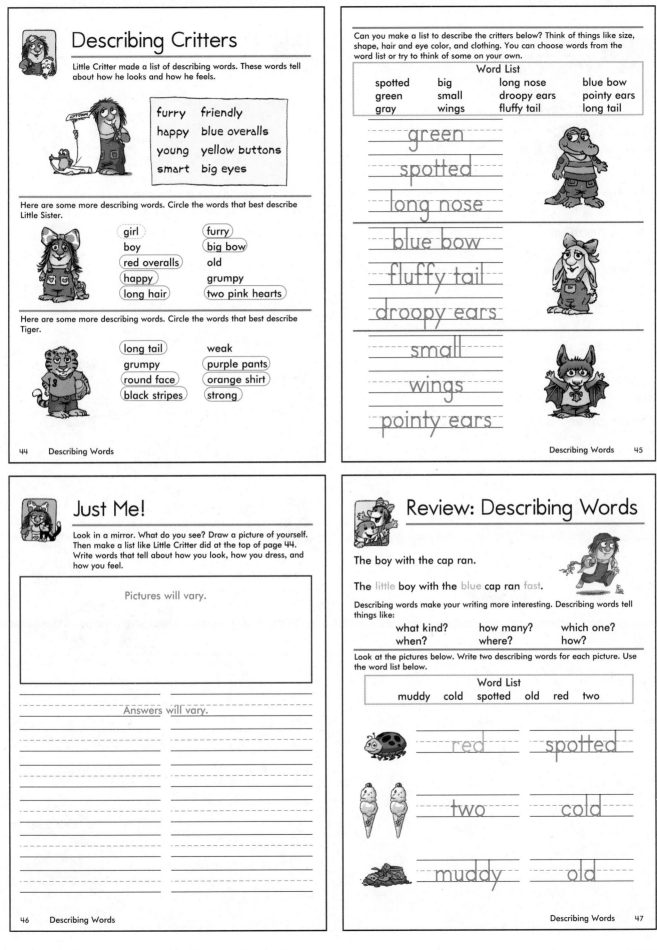

Describing Critters

Little Critter made a list of describing words. These words tell about how he looks and how he feels.

furry	friendly
happy	blue overalls
young	yellow buttons
smart	big eyes

Here are some more describing words. Circle the words that best describe Little Sister.

(girl)   (furry)
boy   (big bow)
(red overalls)   old
(happy)   grumpy
(long hair)   (two pink hearts)

Here are some more describing words. Circle the words that best describe Tiger.

(long tail)   weak
grumpy   (purple pants)
(round face)   (orange shirt)
(black stripes)   (strong)

Can you make a list to describe the critters below? Think of things like size, shape, hair and eye color, and clothing. You can choose words from the word list or try to think of some on your own.

Word List			
spotted	big	long nose	blue bow
green	small	droopy ears	pointy ears
gray	wings	fluffy tail	long tail

green
spotted
long nose

blue bow
fluffy tail
droopy ears

small
wings
pointy ears

Just Me!

Look in a mirror. What do you see? Draw a picture of yourself. Then make a list like Little Critter did at the top of page 44. Write words that tell about how you look, how you dress, and how you feel.

Pictures will vary.

Answers will vary.

Review: Describing Words

The boy with the cap ran.

The little boy with the blue cap ran fast.

Describing words make your writing more interesting. Describing words tell things like:

what kind?	how many?	which one?
when?	where?	how?

Look at the pictures below. Write two describing words for each picture. Use the word list below.

Word List					
muddy	cold	spotted	old	red	two

red   spotted

two   cold

muddy   old

Complete Thoughts

A **sentence** tells a whole idea.

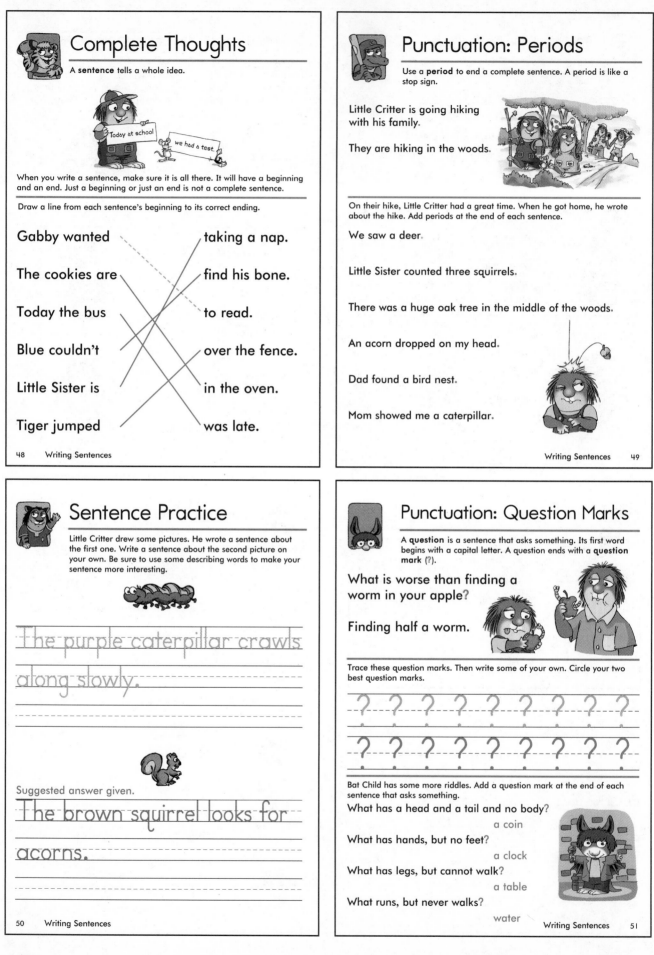

Today at school
we had a test.

When you write a sentence, make sure it is all there. It will have a beginning and an end. Just a beginning or just an end is not a complete sentence.

Draw a line from each sentence's beginning to its correct ending.

Gabby wanted — taking a nap.

The cookies are — find his bone.

Today the bus — to read.

Blue couldn't — over the fence.

Little Sister is — in the oven.

Tiger jumped — was late.

Punctuation: Periods

Use a **period** to end a complete sentence. A period is like a stop sign.

Little Critter is going hiking with his family.

They are hiking in the woods.

On their hike, Little Critter had a great time. When he got home, he wrote about the hike. Add periods at the end of each sentence.

We saw a deer.

Little Sister counted three squirrels.

There was a huge oak tree in the middle of the woods.

An acorn dropped on my head.

Dad found a bird nest.

Mom showed me a caterpillar.

Sentence Practice

Little Critter drew some pictures. He wrote a sentence about the first one. Write a sentence about the second picture on your own. Be sure to use some describing words to make your sentence more interesting.

The purple caterpillar crawls along slowly.

Suggested answer given.

The brown squirrel looks for acorns.

Punctuation: Question Marks

A **question** is a sentence that asks something. Its first word begins with a capital letter. A question ends with a **question mark (?)**.

What is worse than finding a worm in your apple?

Finding half a worm.

Trace these question marks. Then write some of your own. Circle your two best question marks.

? ? ? ? ? ? ? ?

? ? ? ? ? ? ? ?

Bat Child has some more riddles. Add a question mark at the end of each sentence that asks something.

What has a head and a tail and no body?
a coin

What has hands, but no feet?
a clock

What has legs, but cannot walk?
a table

What runs, but never walks?
water

Punctuation Practice

Write a sentence about this picture.

Sample answer is given.

Little Critter has lots of toys.

Write a question about this picture.

Sample answer is given.

Why is Little Critter's room so messy?

Challenge: Write a list of questions that will help you to find out more about someone you already know. Examples: How old are you? What is your favorite food?

Punctuation: Exclamation Points

Sentences that show surprise or excitement end with an **exclamation point** (!). When you read an **exclamation**, your voice should show excitement.

Wow! My tooth came out!

Trace these exclamation points. Then write some of your own. Circle your two best exclamation points.

Little Critter wrote some sentences. Read the sentences or have someone read them to you. Circle the sentences that show excitement. They should end with an exclamation point.

I got a dog for my birthday!

Tomorrow is Monday.

I had a banana for breakfast.

That gorilla ate my banana!

Practice reading each exclamatory sentence with excitement in your voice.

Punctuation Practice

Read Little Critter's story or have someone read it to you. Put three more exclamation points (!) where they belong.

My Lucky Day

One day I was on my way home from school. I was trying to whistle. I had been practicing for a long time, but I could never make a noise. All of a sudden, I could do it! I whistled all the way home.

I played basketball that same day. Our team was tied with the other team. I got the ball and passed it to Gator. He jumped up. Then he dunked the ball through the hoop. We scored the winning basket!

I was walking home from the game and I looked down. I found a shiny, new quarter on the ground. Wow! It was my lucky day!

Punctuation Review

A sentence always begins with a capital letter. It ends with a period (.) or a question mark (?) or an exclamation point (!).

A mouse ran under the table.

Did a mouse run under the table?

Eek! A mouse ran under the table!

Write each sentence. Be sure to use a capital letter at the beginning and a period at the end.

★ i took a red balloon

I took a red balloon.

★ we went to school

We went to school.

★ he played soccer

He played soccer.

★ mom found my glove

Mom found my glove.

★ tomorrow is my birthday

Tomorrow is my birthday.

★ she rode her bike

She rode her bike.

Punctuation Review

Remember to use a question mark (?) when your sentence asks something.

Who jumped over the rock?

Write each sentence. Be sure to use a capital letter at the beginning and a question mark at the end.

★ when are we going home

When are we going home?

★ are you getting cold

Are you getting cold?

★ how did you learn to whistle

How did you learn to whistle?

★ will you get my coat

Will you get my coat?

★ can the dog roll over

Can the dog roll over?

★ where are my shoes

Where are my shoes?

Punctuation Review

Use an exclamation point (!) when you write a sentence that shows surprise or excitement.

Wait for me!

Write each sentence correctly. Be sure to use a capital letter at the beginning and an exclamation point at the end.

★ watch out

Watch out!

★ don't touch that

Don't touch that!

★ look at me go

Look at me go!

★ give me that right now

Give me that right now!

★ he won the race

He won the race!

★ you did a great job

You did a great job!

Sentence Starters

Write an ending for each of these sentences.

The turtle walked to the pond.

Sample answers are given.

I sprayed water on the flowers.

My book is very good.

Riding my bike is fun.

The present was for my mom.

Sentence Starters

Write an ending for each of these sentences.

A big bus took the whole class to the zoo.

Sample answers are given.

The swing was flying high in the sky.

Dad found an old map.

The truck dumped a pile of dirt.

A bad storm woke me up last night.

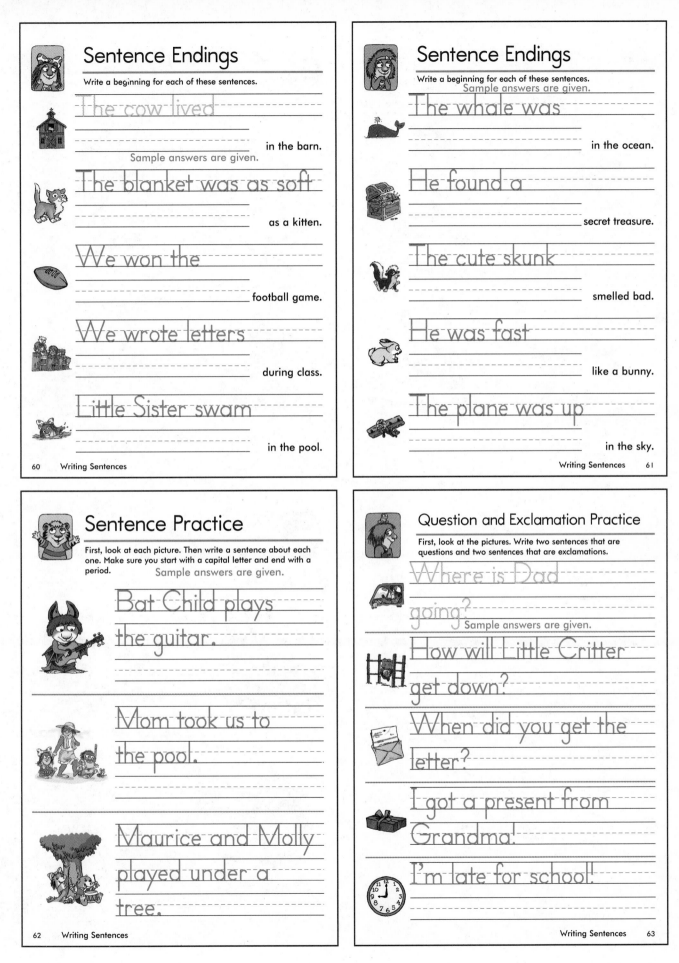

Sentence Endings

Write a beginning for each of these sentences.

The cow lived

___ in the barn.

Sample answers are given.

The blanket was as soft

___ as a kitten.

We won the

___ football game.

We wrote letters

___ during class.

Little Sister swam

___ in the pool.

Sentence Endings

Write a beginning for each of these sentences.
Sample answers are given.

The whale was

___ in the ocean.

He found a

___ secret treasure.

The cute skunk

___ smelled bad.

He was fast

___ like a bunny.

The plane was up

___ in the sky.

Sentence Practice

First, look at each picture. Then write a sentence about each one. Make sure you start with a capital letter and end with a period.   Sample answers are given.

Bat Child plays the guitar.

Mom took us to the pool.

Maurice and Molly played under a tree.

Question and Exclamation Practice

First, look at the pictures. Write two sentences that are questions and two sentences that are exclamations.

Where is Dad going?

Sample answers are given.

How will Little Critter get down?

When did you get the letter?

I got a present from Grandma!

I'm late for school!

Sequencing

Carefully tear out page 65. Cut out the pictures. Match the pictures with the correct sentences. Then glue the pictures to this page.

First, Mom mixed the dough.

Next, Mom cut out the cookies.

Last, she put them in the oven.

Sequencing

Tear out this page. Cut the pictures apart. Put them in order and then glue them onto page 64.

This page is blank for the cutting activity on the other side.

Sequencing

Tear out this page. Cut the pictures apart. Put them in order and then glue them onto page 69.

This page is blank for the cutting activity on the other side.

68

Sequencing

Carefully tear out page 67. Cut out the pictures. Match the pictures with the correct sentences. Then glue the pictures to this page.

First, they got their rakes.

Next, they raked the leaves into a pile.

Last, they jumped in the pile of leaves.

Order Words

Order words tell us what came first, next, and last.

First, Mom mixed the dough.

Next, Mom cut out the cookies.

Last, she put them in the oven.

Label the pictures below **first, next,** and **last.**

next

first

last

last

next

first

Beginning, Middle, and End

All stories have three parts:

beginning	middle	end

Little Sister got out of bed.

She got ready for school.

The school bus took her to school.

Here are three sentences that are not in the right order. Write the sentences in order (beginning, middle, and end) to make a story.

Everyone clapped.

Bat Child did a magic trick.

He made a bunny appear.

Bat Child did a magic trick.

He made a bunny appear.

Everyone clapped.

Using Order Words

Saturday is Little Sister's favorite day of the week. Read her story below and circle the order words you learned on page 70.

First, I help make pancakes. Next, I play all day. Last, I get to stay up until my brother goes to bed.

Using Order Words

Draw a picture about your favorite day of the week. Then write about what you do that day. Be sure to use the order words first, next, and last.

Pictures will vary.

Sentences will vary.

Beginning, Middle, and End

All stories have a beginning, middle, and end. Here are three sentences. They are not in the right order. Write them in order on the lines below to make a story. Then draw a picture of the story.

All of her friends came to the party.

Bun Bun's birthday was Saturday.

They ate cake and played games.

Bun Bun's birthday was Saturday.

All of her friends came to the party.

They ate cake and played games.

Pictures will vary.

The End

Finish this story.

Little Critter and Dad went fishing. They sat in a boat. They waited and waited. No fish were biting. Then, all of a sudden, Dad felt something pull on his line. It was a huge

Answers will vary.

The Beginning and Middle

This story has an ending, but it doesn't have a beginning or a middle. Can you write those parts? Look at the picture and word list for ideas.

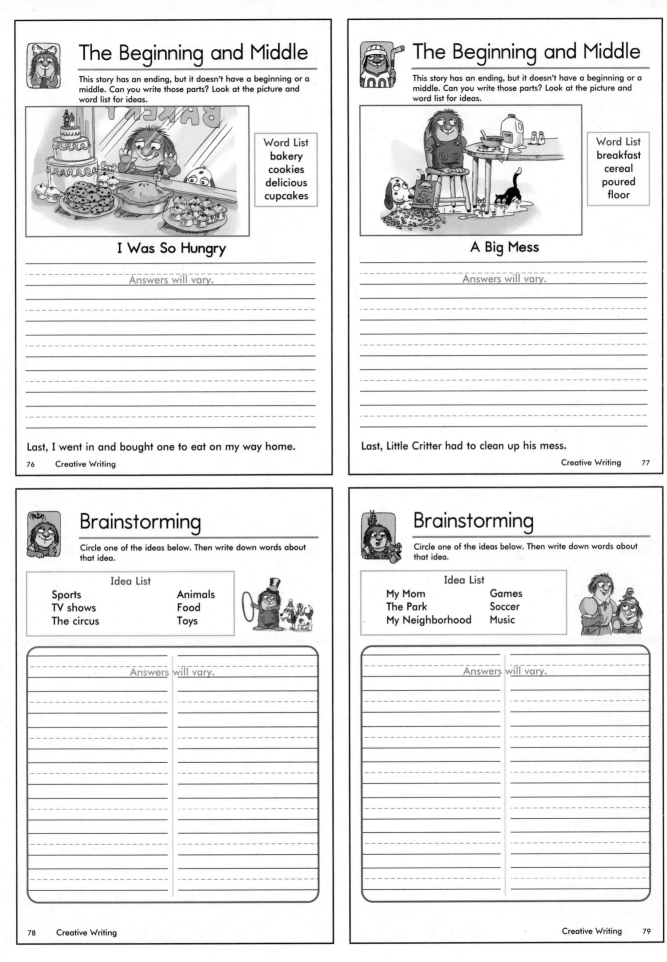

Word List
bakery
cookies
delicious
cupcakes

I Was So Hungry

Answers will vary.

Last, I went in and bought one to eat on my way home.

The Beginning and Middle

This story has an ending, but it doesn't have a beginning or a middle. Can you write those parts? Look at the picture and word list for ideas.

Word List
breakfast
cereal
poured
floor

A Big Mess

Answers will vary.

Last, Little Critter had to clean up his mess.

Brainstorming

Circle one of the ideas below. Then write down words about that idea.

Idea List

Sports	Animals
TV shows	Food
The circus	Toys

Answers will vary.

Brainstorming

Circle one of the ideas below. Then write down words about that idea.

Idea List

My Mom	Games
The Park	Soccer
My Neighborhood	Music

Answers will vary.

Change the Story

Sometimes it is fun to change a story, especially a story everybody knows. Read the story below.

Once upon a time there were three pigs. Each one made his own house. The first pig made his house of straw. The second pig made his house of sticks. The third pig made his house of bricks.

Now write the story again, changing the words in red. Use your imagination. Then read your story aloud to hear the new middle and end you wrote.

Answers will vary.

Follow the Pictures

Here is a story told only in pictures. Can you follow the pictures and write the story below?

Answers will vary.

Follow the Pictures

Here is a story told only in pictures. Can you follow the pictures and write the story below?

Answers will vary.

Just for Fun: Draw and Write

Write a story using one of the ideas below. Then draw a picture to go with your story.

Idea List	
The Day I Learned to Fly	When I Grow Up
I Was So Happy	My Biggest Secret

Answers will vary.

Pictures will vary.

Just for Fun: Draw and Write

Write a story using one of the ideas below. Then draw a picture to go with your story.

Idea List	
One Rainy Day	Going to Outer Space
I Was So Scared	If I Could Be Anybody

Answers will vary.

Pictures will vary.

Just for Fun: Draw and Write

Write a story using one of the ideas below. Then draw a picture to go with your story.

Idea List	
If I Had My Own Zoo	My Best Friend
Three Wishes	I Was So Hungry

Answers will vary.

Pictures will vary.

Writing a Pattern Book

In some cases there is a pattern that the words in a story follow. Only one word changes on each page. Little Critter wrote a pattern book about all the ways he can move. Here are the pages of Little Critter's book.

I can swim.   I can run.

I can roll.   I can slide.

I can jump.   I can climb.

I can walk.   I can skip.

Is this a good title for Little Critter's book?

Things I Can Do

First, write sentences about things you can do. Then read the directions at the bottom of the page to learn how to make a book.

I can _____ Answers will vary. _____

I can _____

I can _____

I can _____

I can _____

I can _____

Make a Book (Book Activity #1)

1. Take two sheets of blank paper.
2. Fold them in half, so the short sides meet.
3. Have an adult staple the pages together or use a sewing machine to stitch up the crease.
4. Write one "I can" sentence on each page.
5. Draw a picture on each page that goes with your sentence. Use interesting colors.
6. Write the title on the front cover.
Now you have a book!

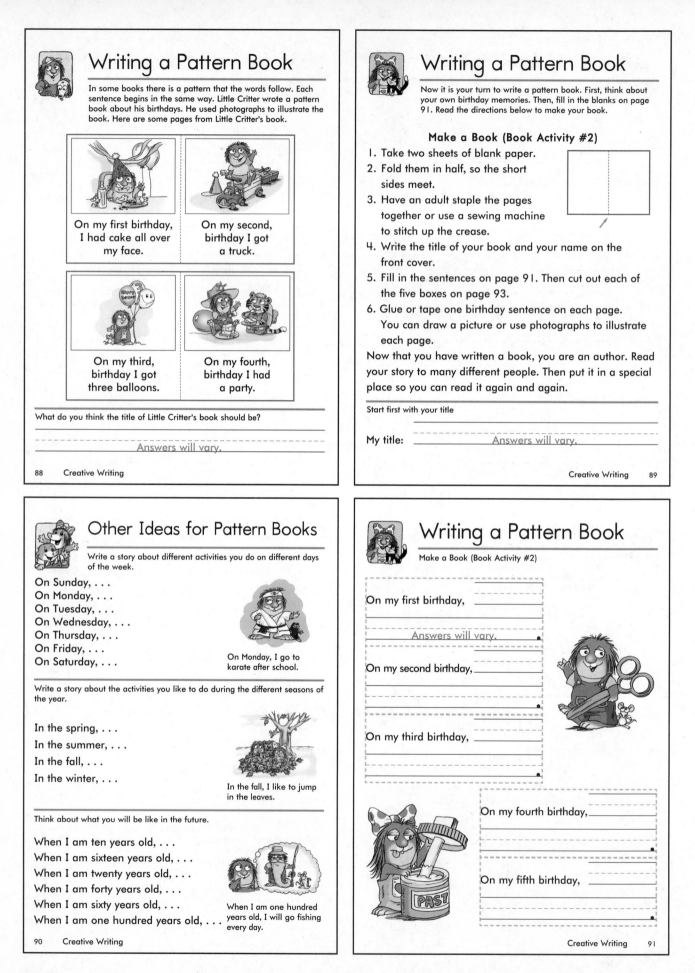

Writing a Pattern Book

In some books there is a pattern that the words follow. Each sentence begins in the same way. Little Critter wrote a pattern book about his birthdays. He used photographs to illustrate the book. Here are some pages from Little Critter's book.

On my first birthday, I had cake all over my face.

On my second, birthday I got a truck.

On my third, birthday I got three balloons.

On my fourth, birthday I had a party.

What do you think the title of Little Critter's book should be?

Answers will vary.

Writing a Pattern Book

Now it is your turn to write a pattern book. First, think about your own birthday memories. Then, fill in the blanks on page 91. Read the directions below to make your book.

Make a Book (Book Activity #2)

1. Take two sheets of blank paper.
2. Fold them in half, so the short sides meet.
3. Have an adult staple the pages together or use a sewing machine to stitch up the crease.
4. Write the title of your book and your name on the front cover.
5. Fill in the sentences on page 91. Then cut out each of the five boxes on page 93.
6. Glue or tape one birthday sentence on each page. You can draw a picture or use photographs to illustrate each page.

Now that you have written a book, you are an author. Read your story to many different people. Then put it in a special place so you can read it again and again.

Start first with your title

My title: Answers will vary.

Other Ideas for Pattern Books

Write a story about different activities you do on different days of the week.

On Sunday, . . .
On Monday, . . .
On Tuesday, . . .
On Wednesday, . . .
On Thursday, . . .
On Friday, . . .
On Saturday, . . .

On Monday, I go to karate after school.

Write a story about the activities you like to do during the different seasons of the year.

In the spring, . . .
In the summer, . . .
In the fall, . . .
In the winter, . . .

In the fall, I like to jump in the leaves.

Think about what you will be like in the future.

When I am ten years old, . . .
When I am sixteen years old, . . .
When I am twenty years old, . . .
When I am forty years old, . . .
When I am sixty years old, . . .
When I am one hundred years old, . . .

When I am one hundred years old, I will go fishing every day.

Writing a Pattern Book

Make a Book (Book Activity #2)

On my first birthday, _____

Answers will vary.

On my second birthday, _____

On my third birthday, _____

On my fourth birthday, _____

On my fifth birthday, _____

This page is blank for the cutting activity on the other side.

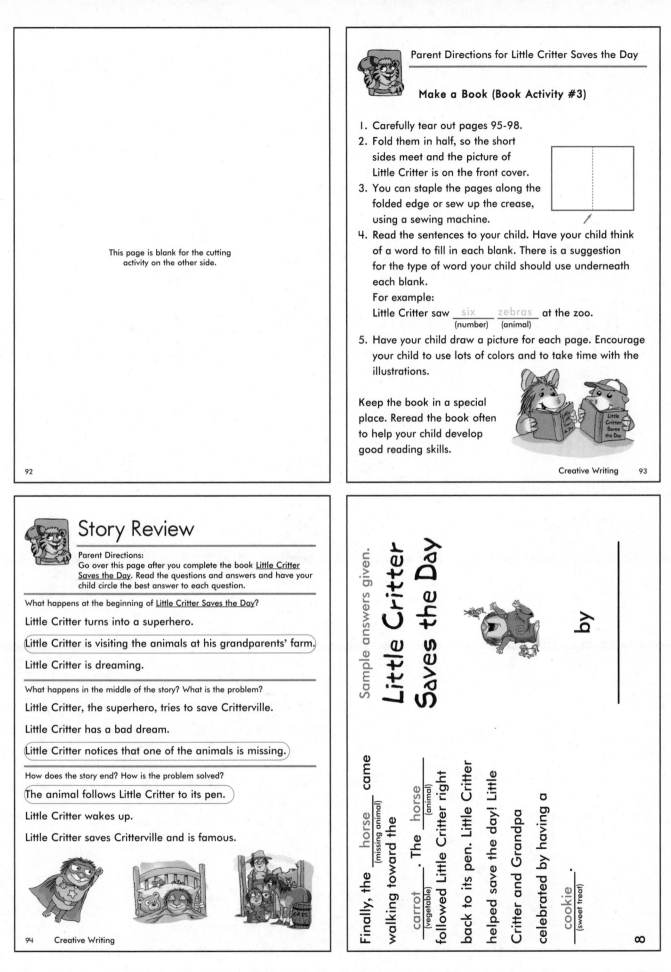

Parent Directions for Little Critter Saves the Day

Make a Book (Book Activity #3)

1. Carefully tear out pages 95-98.
2. Fold them in half, so the short sides meet and the picture of Little Critter is on the front cover.
3. You can staple the pages along the folded edge or sew up the crease, using a sewing machine.
4. Read the sentences to your child. Have your child think of a word to fill in each blank. There is a suggestion for the type of word your child should use underneath each blank.
   For example:
   Little Critter saw ___six___ ___zebras___ at the zoo.
                      (number) (animal)
5. Have your child draw a picture for each page. Encourage your child to use lots of colors and to take time with the illustrations.

Keep the book in a special place. Reread the book often to help your child develop good reading skills.

Story Review

Parent Directions:
Go over this page after you complete the book Little Critter Saves the Day. Read the questions and answers and have your child circle the best answer to each question.

What happens at the beginning of Little Critter Saves the Day?

Little Critter turns into a superhero.

(Little Critter is visiting the animals at his grandparents' farm.)

Little Critter is dreaming.

What happens in the middle of the story? What is the problem?

Little Critter, the superhero, tries to save Critterville.

Little Critter has a bad dream.

(Little Critter notices that one of the animals is missing.)

How does the story end? How is the problem solved?

(The animal follows Little Critter to its pen.)

Little Critter wakes up.

Little Critter saves Critterville and is famous.

Sample answers given.

Little Critter Saves the Day

by _____

Finally, the __horse__ came
          (missing animal)
walking toward the

__carrot__. The __horse__ right
(vegetable)   (animal)
followed Little Critter

back to its pen. Little Critter

helped save the day! Little

Critter and Grandpa

celebrated by having a

__cookie__.
(sweet treat)

8

Little Critter went to his grandparents' farm. He saw a __brown__ (color) __cow__ (animal) .

2

Little Critter walked around the field. He yelled, "Here, __Sammy__ (name) !"

7

3

Next, he went to see the __sheep__ (animal) . Grandma and Grandpa have __five__ (number) of them!

Grandpa asked Little Critter to help find the missing animal.

He gave Little Critter a __carrot__ (vegetable) to give to the __horse__ (animal) .

6

4

Then Little Critter had lunch. Grandma made __pizza__ (food) . It was delicious.

After lunch, Little Critter went to see the __horse__ (animal) . But it was gone!

5

Write Your Own Story

Answer the questions below. They will help you plan your story.

What can happen at the beginning of your story? This is a good place to introduce the people in your story and to tell where those people are.

Answers will vary.

Next, what will happen in the middle of your story? This is a good place to introduce the problem in your story.

Answers will vary.

How will your story end? How will the problem be solved?

Answers will vary.

Once you write down your thoughts, you can make a book. Look at page 87 for suggestions on how to make a book. You can even cut your pages into a special shape. For example: If there is a balloon in your story, cut the pages in the shape of a balloon.

Creative Writing   99

Writing Lists

Making a list is one way to report information or record your thoughts. Little Critter's mom made a list for the grocery store. This is what she wrote.

Grocery List
- milk
- cheese
- bread
- juice
- apples
- cookies

Writing a list is a great way to get ideas for a story. Little Sister made a list of things outside her window. Can you help her finish the list? Use the words from the word list to help you. Be careful — some of the words don't make sense!

Things in my backyard
- trees
- clouds
- squirrel
- airplane
- flowers
- birds
- grass
- leaves

Word List

airplane	birds
spaceship	grass
dinosaur	leaves
flowers	giraffe

Now Make Your Own Lists

Make a list of your favorite foods. Try to think of five things you really like to eat.

Answers will vary.

Make a list of your favorite toys or games. Try to think of five toys or games you really enjoy.

Answers will vary.

Challenge: Use the practice pages in the back of this book to make other lists. Some ideas for lists are:
- things that make you happy
- people you know
- your favorite summer activities
- your favorite stories
- things to buy at the store
- all the animals you can think of
- your favorite movies
- new ice cream flavors

Friendly Letters

Read Little Critter's letter to you below. Look at the four different parts that make up a friendly letter.

1) Date: Begin with a date at the top. Always use a capital letter for the name of the month.

2) Greeting: Start your greeting with **Dear**. Then write the name of the person you are writing to. Begin each word with a capital letter.

3) Body: The body of a letter is what you want to say. Use capital letters to begin each sentence.

4) Closing: You end the letter with a closing and your name. Use a capital letter to begin the closing. Your name should start with a capital letter, too.

September 19, 2001

Dear Reader,

My name is Little Critter. I have a younger sister. Her name is Little Sister. I have a dog named Blue. After school I like to play baseball. What do you like to do after school?

Sincerely,
Little Critter

Parts of a Friendly Letter

Miss Kitty is naming the parts of a friendly letter.

May 2, 2001 — date

Dear Molly, — greeting

I had a good time at your sleep over. Your mom makes the best brownies. The next time, you can come to my house. Thanks again. — body

Your friend, — closing

Little Sister — signature

Name the five parts of the letter below:

January 3, 2001 — date

greeting — Dear Grandpa,

I had a great time visiting your farm last week. You have a lot more animals than I remembered. I hope I can come for another visit soon. — body

closing — Love,

Little Critter — signature

Now it is your turn. Write a letter to Little Critter. Tell him at least two things about yourself. Don't forget to use capital letters.

_____ ,
(Date)

_____ ,
(Greeting)

Answers will vary.

(Body)

_____ ,
(Closing)

(Signature — your name)

Checklist:
I used capital letters for the:
- ☐ date
- ☐ greeting
- ☐ beginning of each sentence
- ☐ closing
- ☐ names

Write a friendly letter to your best friend. Tell your friend about your weekend. Be sure to include all the parts of a letter.

_____ ,
(Date)

_____ ,
(Greeting)

Answers will vary.

(Body)

_____ ,
(Closing)

(Signature — your name)

Checklist:
I used capital letters for the:
- ☐ date
- ☐ greeting
- ☐ beginning of each sentence
- ☐ closing
- ☐ names

Thank You Notes

A **thank you note** is really just a short letter. It tells someone thank you for something. It could be for a gift, a favor, or something nice he or she did.

When you write a thank you note, be sure to include:
- ★ the date you are writing the note
- ★ the person's name in the greeting
- ★ what you are thanking the person for
- ★ your name after the closing

Here is a thank you note to complete. Imagine your grandma sent you $10 for your birthday. Be sure to tell her what you plan to use the $10 for in your note.

_____ ,
(Date)

Dear _____ ,

Answers will vary.

Love,

_____

Thank You Notes

Here is another thank you note to complete. This time imagine your neighbor, Mr. Jones, found your lost dog. Thank him for bringing your pet home safely.

_____ ,
(Date)

Dear _____ ,

Answers will vary.

Your neighbor,

_____

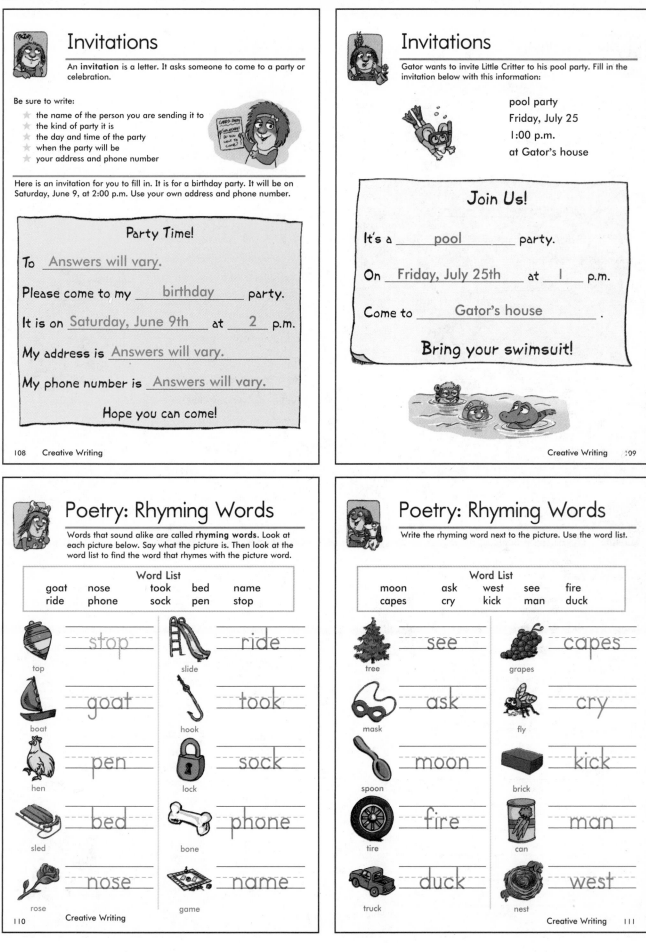

Invitations

An **invitation** is a letter. It asks someone to come to a party or celebration.

Be sure to write:
⭐ the name of the person you are sending it to
⭐ the kind of party it is
⭐ the day and time of the party
⭐ when the party will be
⭐ your address and phone number

Here is an invitation for you to fill in. It is for a birthday party. It will be on Saturday, June 9, at 2:00 p.m. Use your own address and phone number.

Party Time!

To _Answers will vary._

Please come to my ___birthday___ party.

It is on _Saturday, June 9th_ at _2_ p.m.

My address is _Answers will vary._

My phone number is _Answers will vary._

Hope you can come!

Invitations

Gator wants to invite Little Critter to his pool party. Fill in the invitation below with this information:

pool party
Friday, July 25
1:00 p.m.
at Gator's house

Join Us!

It's a ___pool___ party.

On _Friday, July 25th_ at _1_ p.m.

Come to ___Gator's house___ .

Bring your swimsuit!

Poetry: Rhyming Words

Words that sound alike are called **rhyming words**. Look at each picture below. Say what the picture is. Then look at the word list to find the word that rhymes with the picture word.

Word List
goat	nose	took	bed	name
ride	phone	sock	pen	stop

top — stop
slide — ride

boat — goat
hook — took

hen — pen
lock — sock

sled — bed
bone — phone

rose — nose
game — name

Poetry: Rhyming Words

Write the rhyming word next to the picture. Use the word list.

Word List
moon	ask	west	see	fire
capes	cry	kick	man	duck

tree — see
grapes — capes

mask — ask
fly — cry

spoon — moon
brick — kick

tire — fire
can — man

truck — duck
nest — west

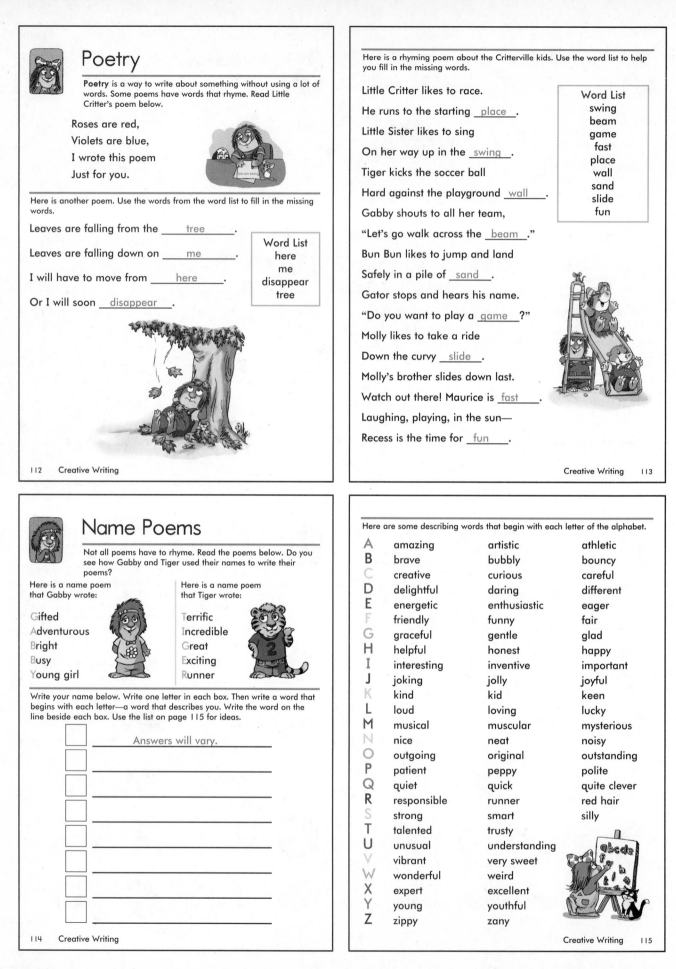

Poetry

Poetry is a way to write about something without using a lot of words. Some poems have words that rhyme. Read Little Critter's poem below.

Roses are red,
Violets are blue,
I wrote this poem
Just for you.

Here is another poem. Use the words from the word list to fill in the missing words.

Leaves are falling from the ___tree___.

Leaves are falling down on ___me___.

I will have to move from ___here___.

Or I will soon ___disappear___.

Word List
here
me
disappear
tree

Here is a rhyming poem about the Critterville kids. Use the word list to help you fill in the missing words.

Little Critter likes to race.

He runs to the starting ___place___.

Little Sister likes to sing

On her way up in the ___swing___.

Tiger kicks the soccer ball

Hard against the playground ___wall___.

Gabby shouts to all her team,

"Let's go walk across the ___beam___."

Bun Bun likes to jump and land

Safely in a pile of ___sand___.

Gator stops and hears his name.

"Do you want to play a ___game___?"

Molly likes to take a ride

Down the curvy ___slide___.

Molly's brother slides down last.

Watch out there! Maurice is ___fast___.

Laughing, playing, in the sun—

Recess is the time for ___fun___.

Word List
swing
beam
game
fast
place
wall
sand
slide
fun

Name Poems

Not all poems have to rhyme. Read the poems below. Do you see how Gabby and Tiger used their names to write their poems?

Here is a name poem that Gabby wrote:

Gifted
Adventurous
Bright
Busy
Young girl

Here is a name poem that Tiger wrote:

Terrific
Incredible
Great
Exciting
Runner

Write your name below. Write one letter in each box. Then write a word that begins with each letter—a word that describes you. Write the word on the line beside each box. Use the list on page 115 for ideas.

Answers will vary.

Here are some describing words that begin with each letter of the alphabet.

A	amazing	artistic	athletic
B	brave	bubbly	bouncy
C	creative	curious	careful
D	delightful	daring	different
E	energetic	enthusiastic	eager
F	friendly	funny	fair
G	graceful	gentle	glad
H	helpful	honest	happy
I	interesting	inventive	important
J	joking	jolly	joyful
K	kind	kid	keen
L	loud	loving	lucky
M	musical	muscular	mysterious
N	nice	neat	noisy
O	outgoing	original	outstanding
P	patient	peppy	polite
Q	quiet	quick	quite clever
R	responsible	runner	red hair
S	strong	smart	silly
T	talented	trusty	
U	unusual	understanding	
V	vibrant	very sweet	
W	wonderful	weird	
X	expert	excellent	
Y	young	youthful	
Z	zippy	zany	

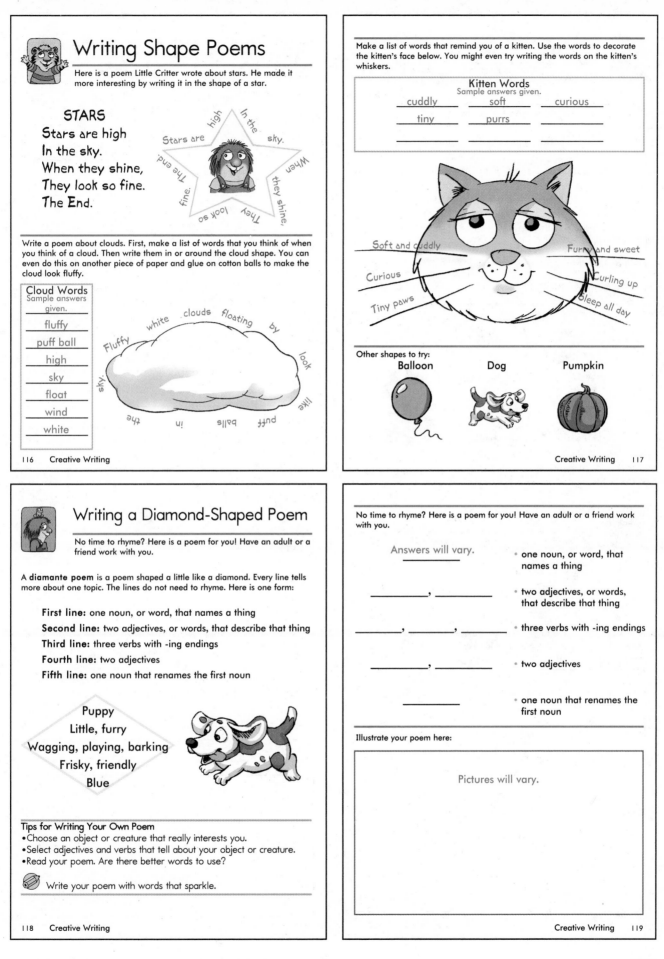

Writing Shape Poems

Here is a poem Little Critter wrote about stars. He made it more interesting by writing it in the shape of a star.

STARS
Stars are high
In the sky.
When they shine,
They look so fine.
The End.

Write a poem about clouds. First, make a list of words that you think of when you think of a cloud. Then write them in or around the cloud shape. You can even do this on another piece of paper and glue on cotton balls to make the cloud look fluffy.

Cloud Words
Sample answers given.
fluffy
puff ball
high
sky
float
wind
white

Make a list of words that remind you of a kitten. Use the words to decorate the kitten's face below. You might even try writing the words on the kitten's whiskers.

Kitten Words
Sample answers given.
cuddly   soft   curious
tiny   purrs

Other shapes to try:
Balloon   **Dog**   **Pumpkin**

Writing a Diamond-Shaped Poem

No time to rhyme? Here is a poem for you! Have an adult or a friend work with you.

A **diamante poem** is a poem shaped a little like a diamond. Every line tells more about one topic. The lines do not need to rhyme. Here is one form:

First line: one noun, or word, that names a thing
Second line: two adjectives, or words, that describe that thing
Third line: three verbs with -ing endings
Fourth line: two adjectives
Fifth line: one noun that renames the first noun

Puppy
Little, furry
Wagging, playing, barking
Frisky, friendly
Blue

Tips for Writing Your Own Poem
•Choose an object or creature that really interests you.
•Select adjectives and verbs that tell about your object or creature.
•Read your poem. Are there better words to use?

Write your poem with words that sparkle.

No time to rhyme? Here is a poem for you! Have an adult or a friend work with you.

Answers will vary.

• one noun, or word, that names a thing
• two adjectives, or words, that describe that thing
• three verbs with -ing endings
• two adjectives
• one noun that renames the first noun

Illustrate your poem here:

Pictures will vary.

Thinking of Things to Write About

Little Critter is making a list of things he can write about. He can use this list when he is searching for an idea for a story.

Things to Write About

★ going to the beach with Grandma

★ spending time at the farm with Grandpa

★ riding the train into the city with Mom

★ going fishing with Dad

★ my pets

★ my favorite teachers

Thinking of Things to Write About

Now it is your turn to start your own list. Remember, you can add to your list whenever you think of something new to write about.

Things to Write About

★ _Answers will vary._

★

★

★

★

★

★

★

More Story Ideas

You can also make a list of things you want to write about by drawing a picture to remember. Little Critter drew this picture of a fun, rainy day. Use the space below to draw pictures of things you would like to write about.

Pictures will vary.

More Story Ideas

Use this page to draw or write about more story ideas.

Answers will vary.

Pictures will vary.

SPECTRUM

SPECTRUM WORKBOOKS
ILLUSTRATED BY MERCER MAYER!

Grades K–2 • 128–160 full-color pages • Size: 8.375" x 10.875" • Paperback

McGraw-Hill, the premier educational publisher for grades PreK–12, and acclaimed children's author and illustrator, Mercer Mayer, are the proud creators of this workbook line featuring the lovable Little Critter. Like other Spectrum titles, the length, breadth, and depth of the activities in these workbooks enable children to learn a variety of skills about a single subject.

- Mercer Mayer's Little Critter family of characters has sold over 50 million books. These wholesome characters and stories appeal to both parents and teachers.
- Each full-color workbook is based on highly respected McGraw-Hill Companies' textbooks.
- All exercises feature easy-to-follow instructions.
- An answer key is included in each workbook.

Wholesome, well-known characters
plus proven school curriculum
equals learning success!

TITLE	ISBN	PRICE
LANGUAGE ARTS		
Grade K	1-57768-840-6	$8.95
Grade 1	1-57768-841-4	$8.95
Grade 2	1-57768-842-2	$8.95
MATH		
Grade K	1-57768-800-7	$8.95
Grade 1	1-57768-801-5	$8.95
Grade 2	1-57768-802-3	$8.95
PHONICS		
Grade K	1-57768-820-1	$8.95
Grade 1	1-57768-821-X	$8.95
Grade 2	1-57768-822-8	$8.95
READING		
Grade K	1-57768-810-4	$8.95
Grade 1	1-57768-811-2	$8.95
Grade 2	1-57768-812-0	$8.95
SPELLING		
Grade K	1-57768-830-9	$8.95
Grade 1	1-57768-831-7	$8.95
Grade 2	1-57768-832-5	$8.95
WRITING		
Grade K	1-57768-850-3	$8.95
Grade 1	1-57768-851-1	$8.95
Grade 2	1-57768-852-X	$8.95

Prices subject to change without notice.

Coming in June 2003!

TITLE	ISBN	PRICE
PRESCHOOL		
Basic Concepts	1-57768-509-1	$8.95
Letters and Sounds	1-57768-539-3	$8.95
Numbers and Counting	1-57768-519-9	$8.95
Reading Readiness	1-57768-529-6	$8.95
Beginning Math	1-57768-579-2	$8.95
Beginning Phonics	1-57768-589-X	$8.95
Beginning Reading	1-57768-599-7	$8.95
Beginning Writing	1-57768-549-0	$8.95

Prices subject to change without notice.

SPECTRUM

Brought to you by McGraw-Hill, the premier educational publisher for grades PreK–12.
All our workbooks meet school curriculum guidelines and correspond to
The McGraw-Hill Companies' classroom textbooks.

TITLE	ISBN	PRICE
LANGUAGE ARTS		
Gr. 3	1-57768-483-4	$8.95
Gr. 4	1-57768-484-2	$8.95
Gr. 5	1-57768-485-0	$8.95
Gr. 6	1-57768-486-9	$8.95
MATH		
Gr. K	1-57768-400-1	$8.95
Gr. 1	1-57768-401-X	$8.95
Gr. 2	1-57768-402-8	$8.95
Gr. 3	1-57768-403-6	$8.95
Gr. 4	1-57768-404-4	$8.95
Gr. 5	1-57768-405-2	$8.95
Gr. 6	1-57768-406-0	$8.95
Gr. 7	1-57768-407-9	$8.95
Gr. 8	1-57768-408-7	$8.95
PHONICS (Grades K–3)/WORD STUDY and PHONICS (Grades 4–6)		
Gr. K	1-57768-450-8	$8.95
Gr. 1	1-57768-451-6	$8.95
Gr. 2	1-57768-452-4	$8.95
Gr. 3	1-57768-453-2	$8.95
Gr. 4	1-57768-454-0	$8.95
Gr. 5	1-57768-455-9	$8.95
Gr. 6	1-57768-456-7	$8.95
READING		
Gr. K	1-57768-460-5	$8.95
Gr. 1	1-57768-461-3	$8.95
Gr. 2	1-57768-462-1	$8.95
Gr. 3	1-57768-463-X	$8.95
Gr. 4	1-57768-464-8	$8.95
Gr. 5	1-57768-465-6	$8.95
Gr. 6	1-57768-466-4	$8.95

Prices subject to change without notice.

LANGUAGE ARTS

Grades 3–6 • 160 full-color pages
Size: 8.375" x 10.875" • Paperback

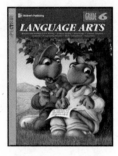

Encourages creativity and builds confidence by making writing fun! Sixty four-part lessons strengthen writing skills by focusing on parts of speech, word usage, sentence structure, punctuation, and proofreading. This series is based on the highly respected SRA/McGraw-Hill language arts series. Answer key included.

MATH

Grades K–8 • Over 150 pages
Size: 8.375" x 10.875" • Paperback

Features easy-to-follow instructions that give students a clear path to success. This series includes comprehensive coverage of the basic skills, helping children master math fundamentals. Answer key included.

PHONICS/WORD STUDY

Grades K–6 • Over 200 pages
Size: 8.375" x 10.875" • Paperback

Provides everything children need to build multiple skills in language arts. This series focuses on phonics, structural analysis, and dictionary skills, and offers creative ideas for using phonics and word study skills in language areas. Answer key included.

READING

Grades K–6 • Over 150 full-color pages
Size: 8.375" x 10.875" • Paperback

This full-color series creates an enjoyable reading environment, even for below-average readers. Each book contains captivating content, colorful characters, and compelling illustrations, so children are eager to find out what happens next. Answer key included.

SPELLING

Grades 3–6 • 160 full-color pages
Size: 8.375" x 10.875" • Paperback

This full-color series links spelling to reading and writing, and increases skills in words and meanings, consonant and vowel spellings, and proofreading practice. Speller dictionary and answer key included.

VOCABULARY

Grades 3–6 • 160 full-color pages
Size: 8.375" x 10.875" • Paperback

An essential building block for writing and reading proficiency, this series extends vocabulary knowledge through grade-appropriate instruction and activities. Synonyms, antonyms, homophones, word families, and word forms are among the key concepts explored. Instruction is based on language arts and reading standards, offering a solid foundation for language arts, spelling, and reading comprehension. The series features a proficiency test practice section for standards-aligned assessment. Answer key included.

WRITING

Grades 3–6 • 160 full-color pages
Size: 8.375" x 10.875" • Paperback

Lessons focus on creative and expository writing using clearly stated objectives and pre-writing exercises. Eight essential reading skills are applied. Activities include main idea, sequence, comparison, detail, fact and opinion, cause and effect, making a point, and point of view. Each book includes a Writer's Handbook that offers writing tips. Answer key included.

TEST PREP

Grades 1–8 • 160 full-color pages
Size: 8.375" x 10.875" • Paperback

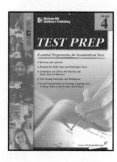

This series teaches the skills, strategies, and techniques necessary for students to succeed on any standardized test. Each book contains guidelines and advice for parents along with study tips for students. Grades 1 and 2 cover Reading, Language Arts, Writing, and Math. Grades 3 through 8 cover Reading, Language Arts, Writing, Math, Social Studies, and Science.

FLASH CARDS

Card size: 3.0625" x 4.5625"

Flash cards provide children with one of the most effective ways to drill and practice fundamentals. The cards have large type, making it easy for young learners to read them. Each pack contains 50 flash cards, including a parent instruction card that offers suggestions for fun, creative activities and games that reinforce children's skills development.

TITLE	ISBN	PRICE
SPELLING		
Gr. 3	1-57768-493-1	$8.95
Gr. 4	1-57768-494-X	$8.95
Gr. 5	1-57768-495-8	$8.95
Gr. 6	1-57768-496-6	$8.95
VOCABULARY		
Gr. 3	1-57768-793-0	$8.95
Gr. 4	1-57768-794-9	$8.95
Gr. 5	1-57768-795-7	$8.95
Gr. 6	1-57768-796-5	$8.95
WRITING		
Gr. 3	1-57768-913-5	$8.95
Gr. 4	1-57768-914-3	$8.95
Gr. 5	1-57768-915-1	$8.95
Gr. 6	1-57768-916-X	$8.95
TEST PREP		
Gr. 1–2	1-57768-662-4	$9.95
Gr. 3	1-57768-663-2	$9.95
Gr. 4	1-57768-664-0	$9.95
Gr. 5	1-57768-665-9	$9.95
Gr. 6	1-57768-666-7	$9.95
Gr. 7	1-57768-667-5	$9.95
Gr. 8	1-57768-668-3	$9.95
FLASH CARDS		
Addition	1-57768-167-3	$2.99
Alphabet	1-57768-151-7	$2.99
Division	1-57768-158-4	$2.99
Money	1-57768-150-9	$2.99
Multiplication	1-57768-157-6	$2.99
Numbers	1-57768-127-4	$2.99
Phonics	1-57768-152-5	$2.99
Sight Words	1-57768-160-6	$2.99
Subtraction	1-57768-168-1	$2.99
Telling Time	1-57768-138-X	$2.99

Prices subject to change without notice.

FIRST READERS

The only first reader series based on school curriculum.

MERCER MAYER FIRST READERS
SKILLS AND PRACTICE

Levels 1, 2, 3 (Grades PreK–2) • 24 Pages • Size: 6" x 9" • Paperback

Young readers will enjoy these simple and engaging stories written with their reading level in mind. Featuring Mercer Mayer's charming illustrations and favorite Little Critter characters, these are the books children will want to read again and again. To ensure reading success, the First Readers are based on McGraw-Hill's respected educational SRA Open Court Reading Program. Skill-based activities in the back of the book also help reinforce learning. A word list is included for vocabulary practice. Each book contains 24 full-color pages.

Level 1 (Grades PreK–K)

TITLE	ISBN	PRICE
Camping Out	1-57768-806-6	$3.95
No One Can Play	1-57768-804-X	$3.95
Play Ball	1-57768-803-1	$3.95
Snow Day	1-57768-805-8	$3.95
Little Critter Slipcase 1	1-57768-823-6	$15.95
(Contains 4 titles; 1 each of the above titles)		
Show and Tell	1-57768-835-X	$3.95
New Kid in Town	1-57768-829-5	$3.95
Country Fair	1-57768-827-9	$3.95
My Trip to the Zoo	1-57768-826-0	$3.95
Little Critter Slipcase 2	1-57768-853-8	$15.95
(Contains 4 titles; 1 each of the above titles)		

Level 2 (Grades K–1)

TITLE	ISBN	PRICE
The Mixed-Up Morning	1-57768-808-2	$3.95
A Yummy Lunch	1-57768-809-0	$3.95
Our Park	1-57768-807-4	$3.95
Field Day	1-57768-813-9	$3.95
Little Critter Slipcase 1	1-57768-824-4	$15.95
(Contains 4 titles; 1 each of the above titles)		
Beach Day	1-57768-844-9	$3.95
The New Fire Truck	1-57768-843-0	$3.95
A Day at Camp	1-57768-836-8	$3.95
Tiger's Birthday	1-57768-828-7	$3.95
Little Critter Slipcase 2	1-57768-854-6	$15.95
(Contains 4 titles; 1 each of the above titles)		

Level 3 (Grades 1–2)

TITLE	ISBN	PRICE
Surprise!	1-57768-814-7	$3.95
Our Friend Sam	1-57768-815-5	$3.95
Helping Mom	1-57768-816-3	$3.95
My Trip to the Farm	1-57768-817-1	$3.95
Little Critter Slipcase 1	1-57768-825-2	$15.95
(Contains 4 titles; 1 each of the above titles)		
Grandma's Garden	1-57768-846-5	$3.95
Class Trip	1-57768-845-7	$3.95
Goodnight, Little Critter	1-57768-834-1	$3.95
Our Tree House	1-57768-833-3	$3.95
Little Critter Slipcase 2	1-57768-855-4	$15.95
(Contains 4 titles; 1 each of the above titles)		

Prices subject to change without notice.

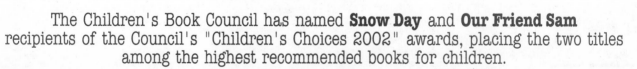

The Children's Book Council has named **Snow Day** and **Our Friend Sam** recipients of the Council's "Children's Choices 2002" awards, placing the two titles among the highest recommended books for children.